EDUCATION AND HUMAN RESOURCE MANAGEMENT

EDUCATION AND HUMAN RESOURCE MANAGEMENT

Dr. (Ms.) Gurpreet Randhawa
Lecturer
Department of Commerce and Business Management
Guru Nanak Dev University
Amritsar

A P H PUBLISHING CORPORATION
ANSARI ROAD, DARYA GANJ
NEW DELHI-110 002

Published by
S.B. Nangia
A.P.H. Publishing Corporation
4435–36/7, Ansari Road, Darya Ganj,
New Delhi-110002
Phone: 011–23274050
e-mail: aphbooks@gmail.com

2026

Typeset by
Ideal Publishing Solutions
C-90, J.D. Cambridge School,
West Vinod Nagar, Delhi-110092

Printed at
DIVINE DIGITAL PRINTERS
Ansari road Daryaganj Delhi-110002

Dedicated To
My Husband
Manbir

PREFACE

The industrial world is becoming increasingly globalized day by day. The organizations are under severe pressure to be innovative and productive so as to remain competitive in the global market. Besides interventions like diversification, technology acquisition and introduction of new systems, it has been observed and also proved by research that eventually much of the result depends upon the human inputs. No wonder, then, that progressive organizations are today more anxious than ever before to get their employees to identify more closely with the organizational objectives and values. Thus it has become necessary for organizations to give special attention to organizational innovation, flexibility, productivity and responsiveness to changing conditions for their survival and success. Moreover, the managers and executives now fully recognize that inculcating a performance-driven culture is the key to success.

Performance is a dependent variable of interest in the study of organizational behaviour because the goals and objectives of the organization are measured in terms of performance or achievement. Work performance is a complex phenomenon that depends on various factors. It is central to any work organization. Numerous studies have been conducted in which work performance was found to be associated with a number of factors. However, a multidimensional approach is required to study work performance. An attempt has been made in this book to assess the interrelationship between work performance and some key variables.

The present book is based upon the research work done as a part of my doctoral dissertation. Here, I want to take opportunity to express my sincere thanks to those people without whom this study would not have been possible. I deem it a pleasure to express my regards and deep sense of gratitude towards my respected research supervisor, Dr. Naresh Kumar, Reader, Department of Management, Kurukshetra University, Kurukshetra, under whose able guidance the present study has been undertaken and completed. His encouraging attitude and personal involvement have been the constant source of inspiration throughout my research work. I am highly indebted to the scientists at the NDRI, Karnal and scientists at the Agriculture Extension Centres in Haryana for their cooperation in data collection and providing me all the necessary inputs required for the present study.

My special thanks go to APH Publishing Corporation for their support in bringing out this book.

I would like to make a special mention of my husband, Manbir Singh Khehra and son, Manraj, who are my source of inspiration and have shown great patience while I have worked on this book. I am also deeply indebted to my parents Dr. S. S. Randhawa and Mrs. Parkash Kaur, for their blessings, inspiration and encouragement, which proved to be a great help. Lastly, I will be failing in my duty if I do not acknowledge my deep indebtedness to my in-laws Prof. Jamail Singh and Mrs. Jagir Kaur for their moral support and help during this work. Thanks are also due to my brother-in-law Kanwal for his support and encouragement.

Any constructive comments and suggestions for improving the contents of the book will be warmly appreciated.

Gurpreet Randhawa

CONTENTS

1

INTRODUCTION

The current economic environment has posed increasing challenges for business and industry to be competitive, both nationally and globally, which in turn, require these organisations to perform better in terms of productivity, quality, time and service. Forward-looking organisations, in such a climate, are taking steps to undergo a massive cultural change so as to bring about corresponding changes in their performance. In this context it would be meaningful to identify and delineate the critical factors in the organisational environment that have the most positive impact on the performance of the enterprise.

The basic objective of organizational behaviour system is to identify and then manipulate the major human and organizational variables that affect the results which organizations are trying to achieve. Managers can only be aware of some of these variables and acknowledge their impact, but for other variables managers can have some control over them. The outcomes are typically measured in terms of various forms of the three basic criteria: performance (e.g. quantity and quality of products and services), level of customer service, employee satisfaction and development.

Since its inception, the microside of organizational behaviour has reckoned individual performance as its primary dependent variable while there is less direct focus on performance in most of the studies; nearly every research write up attempts to draw some implication for management or for current organizational practices. These implications are usually couched in performance terms. Performance refers to a set of outcomes produced during a certain period of time and does not refer to traits or personal characteristics of the performer (Romanoff, 1989).

The declining performance of both private and public sector organisations is of increasing concern to managers, economists, politicians and to all those interested in human performance and productivity in the work setting. Work performance is the degree to which an individual executes his or her role with reference to certain specified standards set by the organisation (Nayyar, 1994). Performance is defined as "observable things people do (i.e., behaviour) that are relevant for the goals of the organisation" (Campbell et al, 1990).

Campbell et al (1993) observed that the concept of performance is poorly understood. They stated that performance is to be distinguished from effectiveness. Performance is synonymous with behaviour, it is what people actually do and it can be observed. Performance includes all those actions that are relevant to the organization's goals and can be measured in terms of each individual's proficiency (that is, his/her level of contribution). Effectiveness, on the other hand, refers to the evaluation of the results of performance and is beyond the influence or control of the individual.

Performance is a dependent variable of interest in the study of organizational behaviour because the goals and objectives of the organization are measured in terms of performance or achievement. In the organization, performance might translate into measures of group task completion, quality and efficiency. On the individual level, performance may be translated into behaviours and actions as rated and evaluated by superiors and colleagues.

Job performance is a fundamentally important construct in organizational practice and research. From a practical perspective, it plays a central role in most personnel decisions, such as merit-based compensation, promotion and retention. It is also used as an important source of developmental feedback. From a theoretical perspective, researchers have long been interested in understanding the causal mechanisms that lead to effective job performance.

Serious attempts have centred around the development of conceptual models seeking explanation for a number of complex but important work-related behaviours. It is abundantly clear that improvization on sophistication of infrastructure, tools and machinery alone does not work until and unless human behaviour-related factors are taken into account - to ensure all-round success. Industrial organizational output is not the ultimate target, more important are the psychological well-being of the work force, their satisfaction, and global development.

Job performance of the employee can be determined by various human and technical factors. The factors that affect job performance include ability and motivation. There is a well-accepted truism that performance is a function of Motivation x Ability (e.g., Campbell et al, 1993). This truism simply captures the logic that ability in the absence of motivation or motivation in the absence of ability is insufficient to yield performance. Ability involves knowledge and skill while motivation is influenced by individual's needs, physical and social conditions. Knowledge involves education, experience, training and interest, while skills relate to aptitude and personality. Individual needs include psychological, social and egoistic needs which embrace general variables. Physical conditions include light, temperature, safety, whereas social conditions include leaders, informal groups and formal organizations.

It has also been emphasized that organizations receive feedback from reviewing and evaluating performance which may be helpful in making adjustments with respect to structures, individuals, groups and other processes (including decision-making and communication). These adjustments are oriented to improve performance through the techniques of organizational change. Thus, for every organizational system, performance appraisal or evaluation is essential.

Performance monitoring – observing behaviour, inspecting output, or studying documents of performance indicators – provides at least subtle cues to employees that their tasks are important, their effort is needed and their contributions are valued (Larson and Callahan, 1990). This monitoring heightens their awareness of the role they play in contributing to organizational effectiveness. Monitoring results alone, however, may not be enough. Many employees are hungry for information about how well they are performing. Without performance feedback – the timely provision of data or judgement regarding task-related results – employees will be "working in the dark" and will not have a true idea how successful they are (Vance and Colella, 1990).

Work performance is a complex phenomenon that depends on various factors. It is central to any work organisation. A number of studies (Hossain, 1997; Lawler and Porter, 1967; Lord and Hohenfeld, 1978; Packard and Thomas, 1989; Schnake, 1991; Vroom, 1964) have been conducted in which work performance was found to be associated with a number of factors. A multidimensional approach is required to study work performance. An attempt has been made in this book to assess the interrelationship between work performance and some key variables (i.e., turnover intentions, job satisfaction and self-efficacy). Attempt is also made to find out the relative contributions of these variables to work performance.

TURNOVER INTENTIONS

Employee turnover has sustained the interest of personnel research, behavioural scientists and management practitioners. Like the study of absenteeism, research on turnover has largely been stimulated by the desire to reduce the cost associated with personnel leaving industrial and government organisations. Turnover has, therefore, been viewed as an important organizational problem. It is important to managers because it disrupts organizational contiguity and is very costly.

Employee turnover can have several negative consequences especially if the turnover rate is high. Often it is difficult to replace the departed employees and the direct and indirect costs of replacing workers to the organization are expensive (Phillips, 1990). The remaining employees may be demoralized by the loss of valued coworkers and both work and social patterns may be disrupted until suitable replacements are found.

An alternative approach to studying the consequences of turnover was suggested by Staw (1980). He noted that turnover has usually been considered a negative outcome variable or cost to be minimized by organizations (e.g. Gustafson, 1982). The costs of turnover such as recruitment, training, and possible disruption of operations are all very real, but they are not the only consequences of turnover. Perhaps very little attention has been paid to the possible benefits emanating from turnover such as hiring someone with greater skills, increased mobility of others in the organization and possible innovation (Dalton and Todor, 1979; Dalton et al, 1981).

Dalton et al (1981) argued for the classification of voluntary turnover as dysfunctional turnover and functional turnover. Dysfunctional turnover means that the individual wants to leave the organization, but the organization prefers to retain the individual. Whereas, functional turnover means that the individual wants to leave the organization and the organization is unconcerned. In this latter case, the organization has a negative evaluation of the individual.

The cost of voluntary turnover depends on many factors, including the relative supply and cost of replacement in either the internal or external labour market, the amount of training invested in employees and the performance level of the employee (Boudreau and Berger, 1985; Cascio, 1994; Dalton et al, 1982). Where replacement costs are low and average performance of the replacement is expected to be high, organizations can benefit from turnover of poor performers. In contrast, turnover of high performers is more likely to be dysfunctional for the organization (Hollenbeck and Williams, 1986; Park et al, 1994). Thus, it is important to identify conditions under which employees of different performance levels are most likely to voluntary leave the organization. However, some benefits may arise from turnover, such as more opportunities for internal promotions and infusion of expertise from newly-hired employees.

Dalton et al (1981) propose that a program to reduce the quantum of turnover may be a shortsighted vision for organizations with relatively large portions of functional and/or involuntary (i.e., unavoidable) turnover; arguably, functional turnover should not be reduced and efforts to reduce unavoidable turnover would be futile. In other words, an organization should focus its efforts on reducing dysfunctional turnover, if possible. Thus, an organization might be able to prevent desirable employees from quitting (dysfunctional turnover) without preventing undesirable employees from quitting (functional turnover).

The employee turnover has been a focus of investigation in several disciplines (e.g. Psychology, Sociology, Economics) for a number of years. Many of these efforts have centred around the development of conceptual models of the turnover process and the subsequent empirical validation of the model. Although these models have diverse origins, several of these have postulated job satisfaction and organizational commitment to be antecedents of turnover. Mobley's (1977) model posits that job and working conditions affect job satisfaction which in turn leads to the thought of quitting, to evaluate the utility of searching behaviour, job search, evaluation of alternatives, comparison of alternatives v/s present job, intention to quit or stay and finally to turnover or retention behaviour. Although it would be unlikely for any single individual to go through all of these decision steps, Mobley's elaboration of turnover as a rational decision process has served as a useful guideline for research (e.g. Miller et al, 1979).

Empirical studies have shown that satisfaction is generally correlated with turnover, but the magnitude of the relationship is not large. Satisfaction, as one would expect, is more strongly related to other attitudes or behavioural intentions than the actual turnover (Mobley et al, 1978) while intentions to quit are more strongly related to turnover (Arnold and Feldman, 1982). The immediate precursor of behaviour is thought to be intentions (Locke, 1968; Mobley, 1977). Therefore, the best predictor of turnover should be the intention to quit (Mobley et al, 1978).

There are at least two intentions of interest in case of turnover behaviour, the intention to search and the intention to quit. Mobley (1977) suggested that the intention to search and search behaviour should generally precede the intention to quit and turnover. Expectations include impulsive behaviour and non-solicited attractive alternatives; an unsuccessful search may lead to form withdrawal other than turnover. Moreover, Staw (1984) highlighted that research on turnover has long utilized models of rational individual decision making. Starting with March and Simon (1958), turnover has been conceived as a conscious process where one evaluates present and future alternatives in deciding to stay or leave the organization. Mobley's (1977) model of turnover, probably the most widely accepted, is a direct descendent of the March and Simon's decision approach.

Early research tended to focus itself on job satisfaction as the key attitude related to employee- behaviours such as job performance and turnover (Locke, 1976). Later research has investigated organizational commitment as an important predictor of employee-behaviour and intentions (Mowday et al, 1982). Wiener and Vardi (1980) suggested that organizational attitudes should be more strongly associated with organizational-oriented outcomes, such as turnover intentions, while the most likely behaviour to be affected by job attitudes would be task-oriented outcomes, such as work effort or performance.

There are areas of research that focus on the process of turnover. The process research has taken an extremely rational decision-making stance, examining the relation between intentions and actions or otherwise testing the cognitive links in the Mobley turnover (e.g. Arnold & Feldman, 1982). Mobley's (1982) model in fact attempts to explicate what leads to turnover intentions precisely because intentions are the immediate cause of turnover. Young blood et al (1983) showed the value of various linkages in understanding this cognitive model of the individual turnover process.

In their model of the turnover process, Arnold and Feldman (1982) show search for alternatives and that tenure and perceived job security are significant factors in influencing the actual turnover decisions.

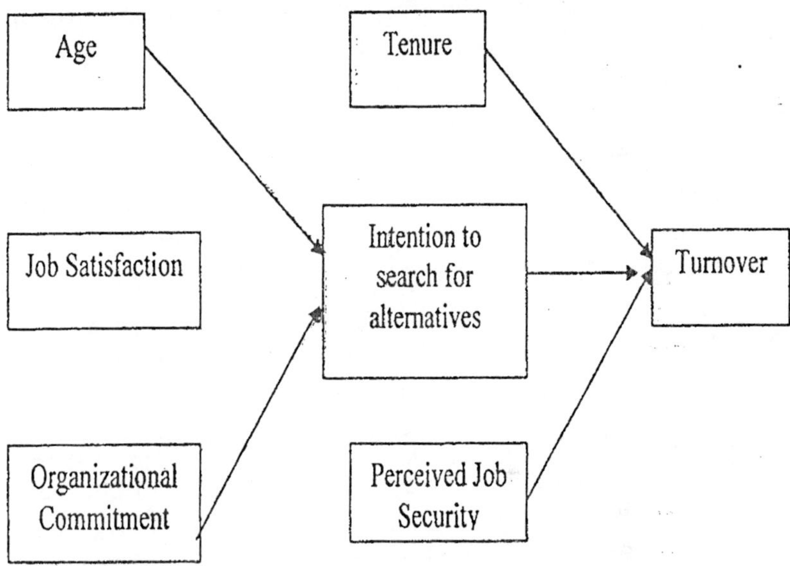

Fig. 1.1 : Model of the Turnover Process

Studies undertaken in the United States by Wotruba and Tyagi (1991) exploring the relationships and reverse causality relationships of certain variables to turnover were used by Brodie (1995) as a basis to identify antecedents of turnover in the United Kingdom and France. Survey results support earlier American findings and confirm that the key variables that contribute significantly to reasons for this high turnover are low-met expectations, poor job image, inadequate job satisfaction and intention to quit.

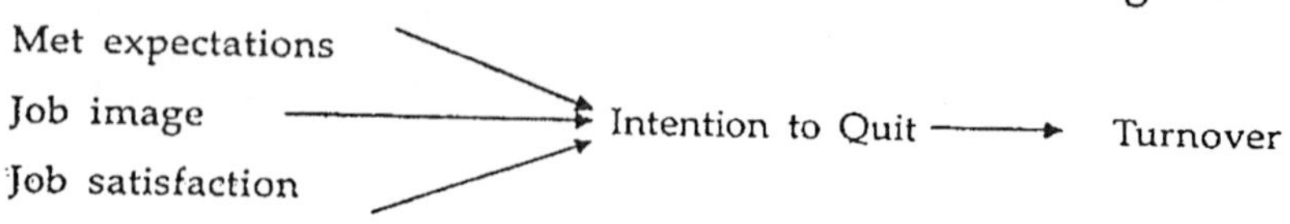

Fig. 1.2 : Antecedents of Turnover

The intent to leave has been identified as the most immediate psychological precursor to actually leaving an organization (Hom & Griffeth, 1995). The intention to leave can be defined as one's behaviour intention to cease working. In their Turnover Model, Wunder et al (1982) also measured intent to leave as a surrogate for actual turnover. Their model was used as a guide for the research of Good et al (1988) who were able to confirm the linkages from the role stressors identified by Wunder et al (1982) to intention to leave by retail managers. They acknowledge, however, that data collection is needed to determine the degree to which intention does predict turnover.

Rusbult & Farrell (1983) have tested an investment model of turnover. Their approach was to monitor how various costs and benefits change for individuals overtime and to examine how these changes are reflected in turnover. They showed that those who left experienced a decline in job commitment over time that was associated with a decline in rewards, an increase in costs and a decrease in investment size, with costs and investments increasing in importance over time. Such results provide support for the idea that turnover is a process and that the process can be monitored.

Steers and Mowday (1981) discussed the importance of understanding the consequences of turnover decision on the individuals making the decision to leave as well as other employees who are observers to the departure. For example, deciding to remain in an organization, though not satisfied, may constitute a dissonance - arousing decision and trigger increases in subsequent satisfaction. Likewise, leaving an organization when one is reasonably satisfied, may cause one to justify the decision after departure. Equally interesting are the consequences of turnover on those who stay in the organization. As Steers & Mowday (1981) noted, those who remain may become dissatisfied simply by watching others leave for other organizations. Such demoralization may be continued by the attribution stayers make about the reasons for leaving.

The consequence of turnover can better be explained in terms of its relationship with performance. The relationship between performance and turnover weights heavily in the determination of whether the organizational consequences of turnover are generally positive or generally negative (Boudreau & Berger, 1985; Hollenbeck and Williams, 1986). An organization that loses a disproportionately high number of its good performers would have more cause for concern than one that loses predominantly poor performers. Mobley (1982) suggested that "the organizational consequences of turnover are dependent on who leaves and who stays."

For several reasons, high performer turnover is more costly at the organization's higher job levels than at lower job levels. For instance, because the standard deviation of performance tends to be greater in more complex jobs (Boudreau, 1992), top performer turnover at higher level jobs results in greater performance losses than similar turnover at lower level jobs. Moreover, performance at higher job levels tends to have a larger effect on firm success and is more difficult and expensive to replace. Finally, turnover of top performers at higher level jobs may result in the loss of future leaders of the organization, suggesting that the importance of top performer turnover in the salaried ranks extends well beyond the short term performance losses and transaction costs associated with such withdrawal.

Several reviews and commentaries have indicated that most researchers have sought either to address methodological issues or to empirically validate existing themes of withdrawal that focus on affect induced quitting (Lee & Mitchell, 1994; O'Reilly, 1991). Lee (1996) suggested that turnover literature would benefit greatly from the introduction of alternative theoretical perspectives that take into account contextual variables surrounding the occurrence of quitting.

A study conducted by Aquino et al (1997) offers such a perspective. They developed and tested a model clarifying the psychological processes by which felt-deprivation instigates quitting. The model draws upon referent cognitions theory (RCT; Cropanzano & Folger, 1989; Folger, 1987; Folger, Rosenfield, & Rheaume, 1983; Folger, Rosenfield, & Robinson, 1983) to explain voluntary turnover. The foundation of their study was examination of relationship between outcome fairness and intentions to quit (Konovsky & Cropanzano, 1991).

The concept of distributive justice is commonly invoked to explain the conditions under which people become dissatisfied with outcomes (Adams, 1965; Walster et al, 1978). According to current theories, fairness judgements are made when people compare what they have received - their outcomes - with those of a referent other (Martin, 1981). This comparison process underlies relative deprivation, or the feeling of discontent arising from a belief that one is getting less than one deserves relative to a comparison other (Crosby, 1984; Martin, 1981). Felt deprivation on the part of individuals produces a range of psychological and behavioural effects in organizations, including dissatisfaction, stress, and absenteeism (Martin, 1981). In general, turnover theorists have conceived "rudimentary" notions of equity (Mobley, 1977) by assuming that distributive injustice in rewards underlies dissatisfaction and ultimately, organizational exits. More recently, scholars have recognized that unfair procedures (Greenberg, 1987; Lind & Tyler, 1988; Thibaut & Walker, 1975) can also stimulate exists (Dittrich & Carrell, 1979; Price & Mueller, 1986).

As per Referent Cognitions theory, people perform three mental simulations involving referent cognitions, justifications and the likelihood of amelioration. Referent cognitions are alternative, imaginable circumstances that differ from a person's actual circumstances. People are most likely to be dissatisfied when the imagined results are more attractive than the existing reality. They become aware of alternatives by discovering that others are receiving rewards different from their own. As referent outcomes are compared to existing outcomes, people think about "what might have been".

The comparison of the referent conditions to the existing conditions provides the basis for justification. For example, if the actual procedures are judged to be inferior to referent procedures, then there will be low justification for existing outcomes. Conversely, superior existing procedures will be associated with high justification. If the rationale for an existing procedure is judged less appropriate or convincing than that for the referent procedure, dissatisfaction will result. When the rationale is considered appropriate, convincing and hence justifiable, dissatisfaction with present outcomes can diminish (Greenberg, 1987; Folger & Martin, 1986; Folger, Rosenfield, & Robinson, 1983).

Research findings of Aquino et al (1997) affirm the powerful effect the interpersonal context can have on employee attitudes and behaviours. The relative strength of the effects of interpersonal and procedural justificaton suggests that the actions of managers rather than the formal structure of procedures tend to elicit the strongest responses from employees. So, they suggested that poor management of employee- perceptions of interactional justice at the supervisory level may ultimately inspire employees to quit. Thus, training and rewarding managers for promoting interactional justice may be a cost-effective way to deter voluntary organizational exit.

JOB SATISFACTION

Job satisfaction is one of the key issues in industrial psychology and behavioural management in organization. It has been a widely researched topic since the beginning of the twentieth century. The factors used to determine job satisfaction have been variously defined by many different researchers. Most studies tend to look at psychological and environmental attributes of job satisfaction. Previous studies also attempted to show the common attributes of satisfaction and dissatisfaction within various industries. Hoppock (1935) defined job satisfaction as any combination of psychological, physiological and environmental circumstances that causes a person truthfully to say : "I am satisfied with my job."

Job satisfaction comprises those outward or inner manifestations which give an individual a sense of enjoyment or accomplishment in the performance of his work. Job satisfaction may come from the product of item produced, from the speed with which it is accomplished, or from other features relating to job and its performance (Roberts, 1966). The term job satisfaction is viewed as a "positive attitude toward one's work, which is global in nature and which results from many specific job-related experiences" (Sharma and Bhaskar, 1991).

A more comprehensive concept of job satisfaction has been formulated by Smith and her associates at Cornell University (1963). According to them, "the feeling of an individual towards the various aspects of his job are not absolute, but relative to the alternative available to him." Locke (1976) described job satisfaction as "a pleasurable or positive emotional state resulting from the appraisal of one's job or job experiences."

In other words, job satisfaction can also be defined as the positive emotional response to a job situation resulting from what the employee wants and values from the job (Locke, 1976; Locke et al, 1983; Olsen, 1993). Blum and Naylor (1968) considered job satisfaction as a resultant of the many attitudes possessed by a worker in different areas.

For an organization to be successful, employers must continuously ensure the satisfaction of their employees. According to Berry (1997) job satisfaction is an individual's reaction to the job experience. There are various components that are considered to be vital to job satisfaction. These variables are important because they all influence the way a person feels about his job. These components include the following : pay, promotion, benefits, supervisor, co-workers, work conditions, communication, safety, productivity and the work itself. Each of these factors figures into an individual's job satisfaction differently. One might think pay is considered to be the most important component in job satisfaction, although this has not been found to be true. Employees are more concerned with working in an environment they enjoy.

Job satisfaction is a complex phenomenon with several inter-related factors personal, social, cultural, economic and organizational. Earlier studies on job satisfaction explored the role of demographic and background factors, besides the predisposing effects of personality variables. These factors influence one's feelings of satisfaction or dissatisfaction with one's work. One of the important factors is age. Researchers have found a positive and linear relationship between age and job satisfaction (Krishnan & Krishnan, 1984; White & Spector, 1987; Lindstorm, 1988). However, some researchers have found the opposite results (Kacmar & Ferris, 1989; Snyder & Mayo, 1991). Herzberg et al (1957) also observed U-shaped relationship between age and job satisfaction.

Good working conditions is also an important factor. Job satisfaction is reduced by overcrowded conditions and dark, noisy environments with extreme temperatures and poor air quality (Sundstrom, 1986). Supervision is another factor. Studies have determined that satisfaction tends to be higher when people believe their supervisors are competent, have their best interests in mind, and treat them with dignity and respect than when they are just the opposite (Trempe et al, 1985). Another factor can be the pay factor. Berkowitz et al (1987) found that the best predictor of job satisfaction was the belief that one is treated in a fair and equitable manner.

It is generally recognized in the organizational behaviour field that job satisfaction is the most important and frequently studied attitude (Mitchell and Larson, 1987). Its importance lies in the fact that while a man is on the work, there are a large number of factors related to work, demographic factors and organizational factors that determine his satisfaction and influence to a great extent the quality and quantity of the output. It has been observed that employee's dissatisfaction with certain conditions of job causes serious industrial problems, whereas employee's satisfaction with job leads to the attainment of the organizational goal of productivity. So, it is a matter of paramount importance to know, whether a person rates himself satisfied or dissatisfied.

Locke (1976) reported that job satisfaction is caused by challenging jobs (high autonomy, stimulation, responsibility etc.), high adequate pay, good opportunities for promotion and good work conditions. He also suggested that the people satisfied with the job are more satisfied with their life, have better physical and mental health and tend to be on the job more frequently and rarely leave the organization as compared to dissatisfied persons.

The sources of job satisfaction and dissatisfaction may vary from person to person. Sources important for many employees include the challenge of the job, the degree of interest that the work holds for the person, the extent of required physical activity, the characteristics of working conditions, the types of rewards available from the organization, the nature of co-workers and the like.

Hulin (1991) stated, "Jobs with responsibility may be dissatisfying to some because of the stress and problems that co-vary with responsibility; others may find responsibility a source of positive affect. Challenging jobs may be satisfying to some because of how they feel about themselves after completing difficult job assignments; others may find such self-administered rewards irrelevant."

There are three important dimensions to job satisfaction. First, job satisfaction is an emotional response to a job situation. As such, it cannot be seen; it can only be inferred. Second, job satisfaction in often determined by how well outcomes meet or exceed expectations. For example, if organizational participants feel that they are working much harder than others in the department but are receiving fewer rewards, they will probably have a negative attitude toward the work, the boss and/or coworkers. They will be dissatisfied. On the other hand, if they feel they are being treated very well and are being paid equitably, they are likely to have a positive attitude towards the job. They will be satisfied with their jobs. Third, job satisfaction represents several related attitudes.

Over the years considerable time and effort have been devoted to discovering the dimensions of job satisfaction. The best conclusion to draw from this work is that, although there are many very specific and diverse job dimensions which are related to job satisfaction, there is a set of dimensions common to most jobs that is sufficient to describe most of the predictable variance in job satisfaction. The size of the set varies roughly from five to twenty job dimensions, but seldom is it necessary to assess the degree of satisfaction using more than ten. The number in this set may vary somewhat depending on the nature of the job and the purpose for which job satisfaction is being investigated.

Smith et al (1969) have suggested that there are five job dimensions that represent the most important characteristics of a job about which people have affective responses. These are : the work itself, pay, promotion opportunities, supervision and coworkers. In a more comprehensive approach, Locke in 1976 presented a summary of job dimensions that had consistently been found to contribute significantly to employees' job satisfaction. Locke (1973) has specified the following job dimensions :

General Categories	*Specific Dimension*	*Dimension Descriptions*
I. Events or Conditions		
1. Work	Work Itself	Includes intrinsic interest, variety, opportunity for learning, difficulty, amount, chances for success, control over work flow, etc.
2. Rewards	Pay	Amount, fairness or equity, basis for pay, etc.
	Promotions	Opportunities for basis of fairness of, etc.
	Recognition	Praise, criticism, credit for work done, etc.
3. Context of Work	Working Conditions	Hours, rest pauses, equipment, quality of the workspace, temperature, ventilation, location of plant, etc.
	Benefits	Pensions, medical and life insurance plans, annual leaves, vacations, etc.
II. Agents		
1. Self	Self	Values, skills and abilities, etc.
2. Others (In-Company)	Supervision	Supervisory style and influence, technical adequacy, administrative skills, etc.
	Co-workers	Competence, friendliness, helpfulness, technical competence etc.
3. Others (Outside Company)	Customers	Technical competence, friendliness, etc.
	Family Members*	Supportiveness, knowledge of job, demands for time, etc.
	Others	Depending upon position – e.g. students, parents, voters.

* Not included in Locke's discussion

The specific dimensions represent those job characteristics typically used to assess job satisfaction. They are relatively specific attitude objects for which the organizational members have some position on a like-dislike continuum. They are also work characteristics salient to most people. For example, consider work itself and pay. Job incumbents quickly form very definite attitudes about the work they do. After very little experience on the job, they have definite feelings about how interesting the work is, how routine, how well they are doing and, in general, how much they enjoy doing whatever it is they do. Likewise, feelings about pay are quite clear. The same amount of pay may lead to quite different feelings about how good it is, but, nevertheless, almost all will have formed for themselves some feeling about that amount.

The general categories of job dimensions are not addressed to by most researchers who attempt to identify the job dimensions important to job satisfaction. Locke (1973, 1976) introduced the general categories in order to cluster common dimensions into more theoretically meaningful groups.

Locke's system is useful, as it provides some basis for considering the adequacy of the set of dimensions as well as a basis for better understanding how and why some dimensions are liked or disliked. For example, according to Locke (1976), "every Event or Condition ultimately is caused by someone or something, and ... every Agent is liked or disliked because he is perceived as having done (or failed to do) something ...".

To the extent that this is so, it is clear that in some settings in which supervisors have considerable control over the work done by their subordinates and over their pay, it is expected that satisfaction with supervision is closely related to satisfaction with the work itself and the pay. In other settings, in which supervisors influence very little the work done by subordinates and subordinates' pay is based upon some companywide scale, then less covariation among satisfaction with work itself, pay and supervision is expected.

It seems intuitively obvious that all job dimensions are not equally important to all people in determining the overall satisfaction with their jobs. Some people may consider their pay very important and working conditions less so; others may consider the reverse. Therefore, when combining measures of satisfaction with several dimensions of a job, it is tempting to weight the dimensions by their relative importance to the particular individual. With few exceptions (e.g., Butler, 1983), the data are very clear for this issue : It does not work (Ewen, 1967). It is much better to select a set of job dimensions that have been found to apply to most jobs and then simply weight each dimension score equally to calculate the overall satisfaction.

Several reasons have been suggested as to why importance rating does not work. The most compelling is that when individuals rate their satisfaction with any single dimension of a job, they also indirectly indicate the dimension's importance (Dachler & Hulin, 1969; Locke, 1976). That an individual has either strong positive or negative feelings about a dimension indicates that the dimension is important enough for that person to feel strongly about it. On the other hand, an individual having neutral feelings of satisfaction usually means that the factor really does not matter much. Therefore, weighting satisfaction ratings by importance is redundant and adds to nothing.

The role played by facet importance is highlighted in Locke's (1969, 1976) theory of satisfaction. Job facets are the individual components that make up one's experience at work (e.g. pay, co-workers, working conditions etc.). Facet satisfaction are affective evaluations of individual job facets. Facet descriptions are affect free perceptions about the experiences associated with individual job facets. Facet description interact with facet importance to determine facet satisfaction. Locke (1969, 1976) observed that workers cannot feel highly satisfied or highly dissatisfied with a facet that is not important to them.

Locke (1969, 1976) suggested an unweighted additive approach to the relationship between facet satisfaction and overall job satisfaction. In this, overall job satisfaction is determined by the simple sum of satisfaction associated with each facet of the worker's job. Locke (1976) asserted that there is no value in weighing facet satisfaction by facet importance when using facet satisfaction responses to predict overall job satisfaction. A number of studies also suggest that job facet satisfaction scores weighted by importance are no better indicators of overall job satisfaction than unweighted job facets (Mikes & Hulin, 1968; Wanous & Lawler, 1972).

Scarpello and Campbell (1983) noted that from a basic research standpoint global job satisfaction is what theories need to predict because (a) the variety of facets that are potentially predictable is great and (b) the sum of the facets does not appear to be the same as the results obtained from global measure.

SELF-EFFICACY

With the development of micro-analytic methodology for testing propositions about the origins and functions of perceived self-efficacy (Bandura, 1977), research attempts were addressed to the processes governing the interrelationship between knowledge/skill and action. It has been a point of common observation that knowledge, transformational operations and component skills are necessary but insufficient for accomplished performances. Indeed, people often do not perform optimally, even though they know well what to do. This is because self-referent thought also mediates the relationship between knowledge and action (Bandura, 1982). It becomes important to know how people judge their capabilities and how through their self-percepts of efficacy, they affect their behavioural outcomes.

The theoretical construct which now regularly appears in the literature of industrial and organizational psychology was previously first defined in social psychology. The concept of self-efficacy was first of all put forth and developed by Albert Bandura (1977, 1982, 1986). Self-efficacy is a key concept in Bandura's social-learning theory (Bandura, 1977).

Bandura (1986) defined self-efficacy as "people's judgements of their capabilities to organize and execute courses of action required to attain designated types of performances". In other words, self-efficacy is a person's belief about his or her chances of successfully accomplishing a specific task. It is belief in one's ability to do a task. Self-efficacy arises from the gradual acquisition of complex, cognitive, social, linguistic, and/or physical skills through experience (Bandura, 1977; Gist, 1987; Gist & Mitchell, 1992) whereas Wood and Bandura (1989) stated that "self-efficacy refers to beliefs in one's capabilities to mobilize the motivation, cognitive resources and courses of action needed to meet given situational demands."

An individual with high self-efficacy has more confidence in his ability to succeed in a task. It is observed that in difficult situations, people with low self-efficacy are more likely to lessen their effort or give up altogether, while those with high self-efficacy will try harder to master the challenge (Locke et al, 1984). In addition, individuals high in self-efficacy, seem to respond to negative feedback with increased effort and motivation, whereas those low in self-efficacy are likely to lessen their effort when given negative feedback (Bandura, 1986).

Bandura's self-efficacy theory provides explicit guidelines on how to develop and enhance human efficacy. In the exercise of human agency, the most central or pervasive mechanism of personal agency through which people make causal contributions to their own psychosocial functioning is people's beliefs in personal efficacy. Efficacy beliefs influence how people think, feel, motivate themselves and act, for the diverse causal tests consistently show that such beliefs contribute significantly to human motivation and attainments.

Self-efficacy is a construct derived from social-cognitive theory – a theory positing a triadic reciprocal causation model in which behaviour, cognitions and the environment all influence each other in a dynamic fashion (Bandura, 1977, 1986). Bandura suggested that four categories of experience are used in the development of self-efficacy. The foremost and most effective way of creating a strong sense of efficacy is through mastery experiences and these provide the most reliable testimony whether one can mobilize whatever it takes to supervene (Bandura, 1982; Biran & Wilson, 1981; Feltz et al, 1979; Gist, 1989). Successes help in building a sound belief in one's personal efficacy. Failures can prove hurdle, especially if they occur before a sense of efficacy is firmly established. Development of self-efficacy through this method involves acquiring the cognitive, behavioural and self-regulatory tools for creating and executing appropriate courses of action in order to manage ever changing life-circumstances.

The second influential way of creating and strengthening efficacy is vicarious experiences (modeling) provided by social models. Seeing people similar to themselves succeed by perseverant effort raises observers' beliefs that they too possess the capabilities to master comparable activities (Bandura, 1986; Schunk, 1987). In the same way, observing others fail despite high effort lowers observers' judgements of their own efficacy and undermines their level of motivation (Brown & Inouye, 1978). Thus, the impact of modeling on personal efficacy beliefs is greatly and strongly influenced by the perceived similarity to the models.

Social persuasion is the third way of strengthening people's beliefs about their success. People who are persuaded verbally that they possess the capabilities to master given activities are likely to mobilize greater effort and sustain it, than if they harbour self-doubts and abide by personal deficiencies when problems arise (Litt, 1988; Schunk, 1989). It is observed that it is more difficult to instill high beliefs in personal efficacy by social persuasion alone than to undermine them.

The fourth way of strengthening people's belief that they have in them what it takes to succeed is their own physiological and emotional states in estimating their capabilities. People often take their stress reactions and tensions as signs of susceptibility to poor performance. In activities involving strength and stamina, people judge their fatigue, aches and pains as signs of physical debility (Ewart, 1992). An important role is also played by mood in affecting people's judgements of their personal efficacy. Where positive mood enhances perceived self-efficacy; despairing mood diminishes it (Kavanagh & Bower, 1985). Perception and interpretation of emotional and physical reactions are more important than their sheer intensity; for example, people possessing a high sense of efficacy are likely to perceive their state of affective arousal as an energizing facilitator of performance, whereas people preoccupied with self-doubts regard their arousal as a debilitator. Thus, physiological indicators of efficacy play an influential role in health functioning and in activities requiring physical strength and stamina.

Although these experiences influence efficacy perceptions, it is the individual's cognitive appraisal and integration of these experiences that ultimately determine self-efficacy (Bandura, 1982). The efficacy beliefs regulate human functioning through four major processes. These are cognitive, motivational, affective and selection processes which operate collectively rather than in isolation.

Efficacy beliefs affect the cognitive processes in various forms. Human behaviour being purposive is governed by forethought embodying valued goals. Self-appraisal of capabilities influences the personal goal setting. The stronger the perceived self-efficacy, the higher the goal challenges people set for themselves and the firmer is their commitment to them (Locke & Latham, 1990).

The actions to be undertaken in course of time are initially organized in thoughts. Efficacy beliefs which people hold, guide and shape the future course of action which people construct and rehearse. People holding high personal efficacy beliefs visualize success and this positively guides and supports them for performance. People who doubt their efficacy visualize failure and do things that can go wrong because it becomes very difficult to achieve anything while fighting self-doubts. The main thing is that thoughts facilitate in predicting events and to acquire skills to control those events which affect lives. All this can be most effectively done through effective cognitive processing of information that contains numerous uncertainties, doubts and complexities.

Wood and Bandura (1989) observed that in the most pressing situational demands, failures, a strong sense of efficacy is required to overcome these. Specially they observed that under most taxing circumstances people possessing low self-efficacy become more and more inconsistent in their analytic thinking and lower their aspirations resulting in poor performance in contrast to people who with a high robust sense of efficacy set high goals and achieve them with proud possession of their efficacy beliefs.

Self-regulation of motivation is the other area in which self-efficacy beliefs are said to be effective. It is seen that each and every action of an individual is the outcome of all the anticipations he holds while setting goals and planning a future course of action. In order to attain the set goals, the available resources are mobilized to the maximum. Human motivation is mostly cognitively generated and there are three different forms of cognitive motivators around which different theories have been developed. These three form are – causal attributions, outcome experiences and cognized goals. Efficacy beliefs are seen to be operative in all these types of cognitive motivation.

Another area where self-efficacy beliefs are effective is affective processes. It is the self-efficacy belief an individual possesses which determines how he or she copes with stressful and depressing situations. Bandura (1991) concluded that perceived self-efficacy to exercise control over stresses plays a key role in anxiety arousal.

The fourth area in which self-efficacy beliefs are said to be effective is selection process. People are partly the product of their environment and their efficacy beliefs can help them in choosing the type of activities and environments they wish to get into and, thus, shaping the course their lives take. People with a high sense of efficacy avoid activities and select environments they believe exceed their coping capabilities. But they readily undertake challenging activities and select environments they judge themselves capable of managing.

Those who have a low sense of efficacy in given domains shy away from difficult tasks, which they view as personal threats. They have low aspirations and weak commitment to the goals they choose to pursue. When faced with difficult tasks, they dwell on their personal deficiencies, the obstacles they are likely to face and all kinds of adverse outcomes rather than concentrate on how to perform successfully. They tend to decrease their effort and surrender easily in the face of difficulties and if they face setbacks then they are very slow to recover their sense of efficacy and easily fall prey to stress and depression.

In contrast to it, a person with a high sense of efficacy enhances human accomplishment and personal well-being in many ways. Such a person accepts difficult jobs as challenges to be mastered rather than threats to be avoided. Such ruminations and attitudes foster intrinsic interest and deep engrossment in activities. They heighten and sustain his efforts in the face of difficulties and tend to quickly recover his sense of efficacy after failures or setbacks and attribute failure to insufficient effort or to deficient knowledge and skills that are acquirable.

Strong efficacy beliefs are not produced merely by verbally proclamations, rather these are the product of a complex process of self persuasion that relies on cognitive processing of diverse sources of efficacy information which once formed improve the quality of human life to a great extent.

Organizational psychologists have followed Bandura (1986) in focusing on specific self-efficacy (SSE), largely ignoring general self-efficacy (GSE). SSE is a situational specific cognition that is focused on a particular task. Studying it requires devising an ad hoc measure for each task; such measures are rarely used twice. Self-efficacy field researchers have measured and raised such narrowly focused SSE as, "attendance-self-efficacy", "job seeking self-efficacy", and "software self-efficacy" (Caplan et al, 1989; Frayne & Latham, 1987; Gist et al, 1989).

Perceived self-efficacy is concerned with judgements of how well one can execute courses of action required to deal with prospective situations. Competency belief as referred to by Wood and Locke (1987) can stem from many sources including attributions about the causes of previous attainments and perceptions of ability, adaptability, creativity and capacity for self-control. Perceived self-efficacy can be defined as an individual's estimate of his or her capability of performing a specific set of actions required to deal with task-situations. Self-efficacy is hypothesized to be an important determinant of action and, therefore, given the appropriate level of skill, performance (Bandura, 1982, 1986).

According to Bandura, self-efficacy is causally related to action independently of the individual's actual demonstrated ability on a task, even though the two are related. Thus, the same degree of actual success in performing a task can lead to different degrees of experienced self-efficacy, because different individuals may reach different conclusions from the same previous attainment. For example, one person may succeed but not really feel in control of the task, because it was very hard or because he or she felt very nervous, whereas another may find achieving the same degree of success to be effortless. So, the subsequent performance of the task will have the reflection of these different percepts of self-efficacy.

In order to illustrate the causal power of self-efficacy, Bandura and his colleagues have conducted experiments in different settings (e.g. Bandura, 1982; Bandura & Cervone, 1986; Bandura & Schunk, 1981). The level of performance, task choice, effort, persistence and stress-reactions are found to be influenced by this.

Self-efficacy is seen in helping people in exercising control over events that affect their lives. People are able to realize desired goals and to forestall undesired ones with the help of the process of exerting influence in spheres over which they can exercise some control. There is a strong desire (longing) to have control over life-circumstances and this desire permeates almost everything people do because it can accompany innumerable personal and social benefits. The ability to affect outcomes makes them predictable and this predictability results into adoptive preparedness, whereas the inability to exert influence over things that adversely affect one's life breeds apprehension, apathy or despair. So, the capability to produce valued outcomes and to prevent undesired ones provides powerful incentives for the development and exercise of personal control.

Because of the centrality of control in human lives, various theories about self-efficacy have been propounded over the years (Adler, 1956; DeCharms, 1978; Rotter, 1966; White, 1959). People's level of motivation, affective states and actions are based more on what they believe in than on what is objectively the case. Thus, the beliefs people hold for their causative capabilities are to be inquired and to fully understand the causative reason, origin, structure, function, effects and processes through which they operate should be studied. Self-efficacy theory addresses itself to all of these sub-processes both at the individual and collective level.

There has been a growing convergence of theory and research in recent years on the influential role of self-efficacy and self-referent thought in performance accomplishments and other outcome-related behaviours (e.g. Waldersee, 1994; Lindsley et al, 1995). Though the researches have been undertaken from a number of different perspectives assuming a variety of names, yet the basic phenomenon being addressed to centres on people's sense of personal efficacy to produce and to regulate events in their lives.

The variety of perspectives includes the mediating role of self-efficacy in the organizational performance (Lindsley et al, 1995; Sanna & Pusecker, 1994), contribution to the prediction of vocational congruence (Luzzo & Ward, 1995), moderating effect on stress reactions (Saks, 1995), collective efficacy and working together at work-place (Parker, 1994), performance in sports (Miller, 1993) and scholastic achievement (Vasil, 1993).

Empirical studies of self-efficacy have yielded several consistent findings e.g., self-efficacy is associated with work-related performance : life insurance sales (Barling & Beattie, 1983), faculty research productivity (Taylor et al, 1984), coping with difficult career-related tasks (Stumpf et al, 1987), career choice (Campbell & Hackett, 1986; Wood & Locke, 1987) and adaptability to new technology (Hill et al., 1987).

Bandura (1986) has also asserted that self-efficacy is significantly and positively related to future performance and extensive research strongly supports this claim. Besides, it is considered to be a significant variable in goal-setting theory (Locke & Latham, 1990). Over the past few years, research has demonstrated a clear connection between self-efficacy and behaviour. First, it has been found that self-efficacy influences our choice of actions (Bandura, 1977). We avoid tasks we do not think we are up to, and choose those which we assume ourselves capable of accomplishing. It should be emphasized here that it is the expectations which have the effect – not our ability or lack of ability to cope with the task.

Second, self-efficacy affects the amount of energy we invest in a task, and the length of time during which we perservere without achieving the desired results (Bandura & Schunk, 1981; Brown et al, 1989; Bouffard–Bouchard, 1990). Individuals with low self-efficacy invest less and give up sooner. Third, self-efficacy affects our performance. Tasks located within an experienced "area of confidence" are carried out successfully, while tasks outside it create problems (Bandura, 1977). Corresponding results have been demonstrated in a number of other experiments. Self-efficacy affects both motivation and performance (Barling & Beattie, 1983; Bouffard–Bouchard, 1990; Brown et al, 1989; Hackett & Betz, 1989; Robertson & Sadri, 1993; Shell et al, 1989; Taylor et al, 1984).

HOW SELF-EFFICACY BELIEFS CAN PAVE THE WAY FOR SUCCESS OR FAILURE

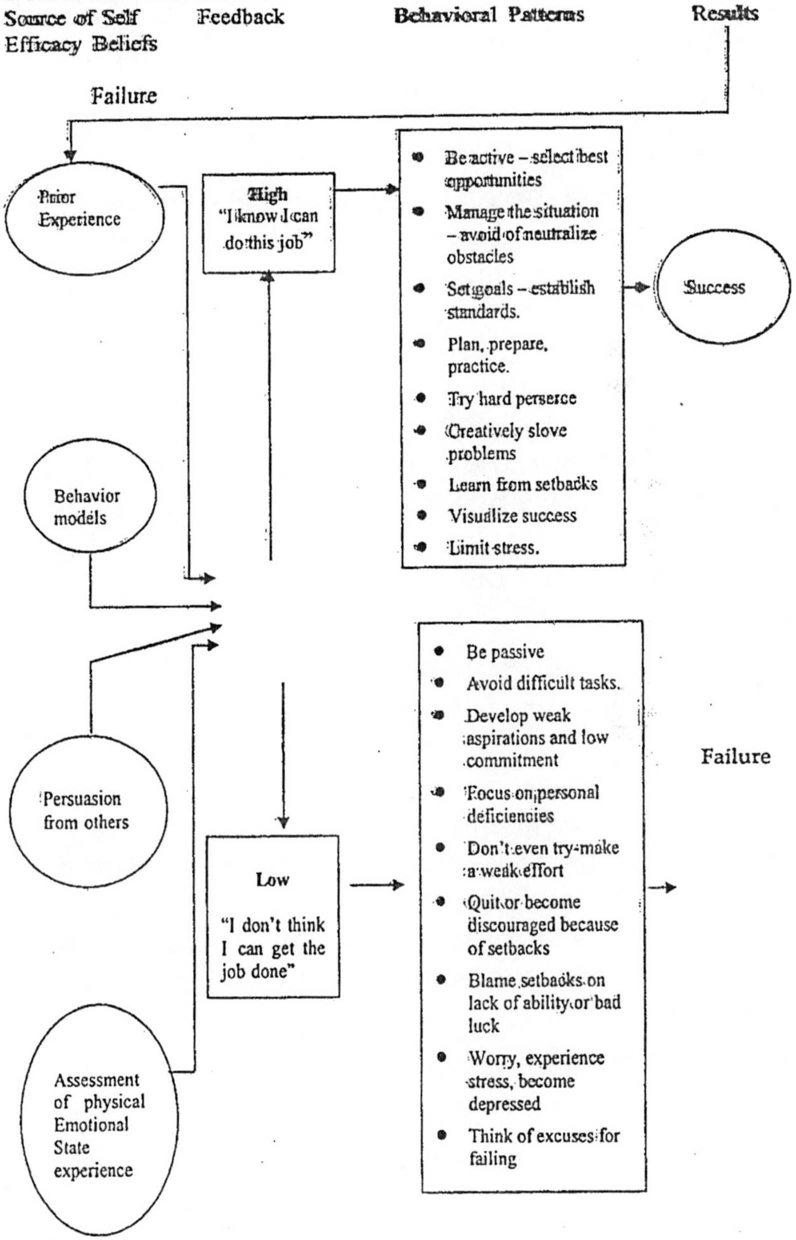

Source of Self Efficacy Beliefs

Feedback

Behavioral Patterns

Results

Failure

Prior Experience

Behavior models

Persuasion from others

Assessment of physical Emotional State experience

High
"I know I can do this job"

- Be active – select best opportunities
- Manage the situation – avoid of neutralize obstacles
- Set goals – establish standards.
- Plan, prepare, practice.
- Try hard perserce
- Creatively slove problems
- Learn from setbacks
- Visualize success
- Limit stress.

Success

Low
"I don't think I can get the job done"

- Be passive
- Avoid difficult tasks.
- Develop weak aspirations and low commitment
- Focus on personal deficiencies
- Don't even try-make a weak effort
- Quit or become discouraged because of setbacks
- Blame setbacks on lack of ability or bad luck
- Worry, experience stress, become depressed
- Think of excuses for failing

Failure

The model depicts that your self-efficacy calculation would involve cognitive appraisal of the interaction between your persevered capability and situational opportunities and obstacles. As you begin to prepare for some task, the four sources of self-efficacy belief come into play. Because prior experience is the most potent source, it is listed first and connected to self-efficacy beliefs with a solid line (Rubin et al, 1993). Past success on a similar task would boost your self-efficacy. But bad experiences with similar tasks would foster low self-efficacy. Regarding behaviour models as a source of self-efficacy belief, you would be influenced by the success or failure of your colleagues in similar tasks. Their success would tend to bolster you, likewise any supportive persuasion from your classmates that you will do a good job would enhance your self-efficacy. Physical and emotional facts might also affect your self-confidence. Your cognitive evaluation of the situation then would yield a self-efficacy belief ranging from high to low expectation of success.

Moving to the behavioural-patterns portion in the model, we see how self-efficacy beliefs are acted out. In short, if you have high self-efficacy about your task, you will work harder, more creatively and longer while preparing for the task to be undertaken immediately. The results would then take shape accordingly. People program themselves for success or failure by enhancing their self-efficacy expectations. Positive or negative results subsequently become feedbacks for one's base of personal experience.

OBJECTIVES AND PLAN OF THE BOOK

Work in today's organizations is characterized by increasing complexity, rapid change and increasingly competitive business environments (Cascio, 1998; Goldstein, 1993; Smith et al, 1997). Thus, a critical issue in work settings that has been agitating the minds of all concerned including behavioural scientists, economists and management practitioners and even managers and workers is to get maximum work output with available human potential at a work place. Efforts have been made independently and jointly by all concerned to explore the role of organization-related and a number of work-relevant behaviours of employees. Particularly, behavioural scientists have been concentrating on certain psychological predispositions and other work-relevant behaviours. Out of the many variables such as psychological variables, dispositional characteristics and some organizational variables such as job specific self-efficacy, job satisfaction and turnover intentions have been studied as predictors of job performance. Most of the earlier research attempts concentrated on investigating the relationship between job performance and turnover intentions, job satisfaction and self-efficacy separately. Moreover, majority of studies concentrated on bivariate approach which does not account for relative contribution of well known antecedents of work performance. Thus considering the theoretical and applied importance of the concepts of turnover intentions, job satisfaction and self-efficacy, the present study has been proposed.

The main objectives of the study are :

1. To study the relationship between turnover intentions and work performance.
2. To study the relationship between job satisfaction and work performance.
3. To study the relationship between self-efficacy and work performance.
4. To study the effect of turnover intentions on work performance.

5. To study the effect of job satisfaction on work performance.
6. To study the effect of self-efficacy on work performance.
7. To study the joint contribution of turnover intentions, job satisfaction and self-efficacy on work performance.

2

STUDIES ON WORK PERFORMANCE

The review of the related literature has been presented under following headings i.e. turnover intentions and job performance, job satisfaction and job performance, self-efficacy and job performance, job satisfaction and turnover intentions, self-efficacy and job satisfaction.

TURNOVER INTENTIONS AND JOB PERFORMANCE

Research on employee turnover since the Porter & Steers (1973) analysis of the literature reveals that age, tenure, overall satisfaction, job content, intentions to remain on the job and commitment are consistently and negatively related to turnover. Generally, however, less than 20% of the variance in turnover is explained.

The Fishbein (1967) model of the relationships among beliefs, attitudes, intentions and behaviours emphasizes the role of intentions in understanding the link between attitudes and behaviour. The Locke (1968) model of task motivation also conceives of intention as an immediate precursor of behaviour. Drawing on these and other related theoretical models, a number of recent studies have assessed the role of intentions in predicting and understanding turnover. These studies indicate that behavioural intentions to stay or leave are consistently related to turnover behaviour.

Turnover intention has been assumed and found to be the only antecedent having a direct effect on actual turnover

(Coverdale & Terborg, 1980; Fishbein & Ajzen, 1974; Michaels & Spector, 1982; Miller et al, 1979; Mobley, 1977; Mobley et al, 1978; Mowday et al, 1984). After reviewing the literature on the employee turnover processes, Mobley et al (1979) concluded, "behavioral intentions to stay or leave are consistently related to turnover behaviour." Indeed, turnover intention has consistently been demonstrated to have a significant and positive relationship with turnover, with the average coefficient being +.38 (Carsten & Spector, 1987). On the other hand, such a relationship has not been found between different types of withdrawal behaviour (such as lateness and voluntary absence) and actual turnover (Miller, 1981, 1982).

Research studies indicate that the perceived intrinsic value of work, intrinsic motivation, and intrinsic satisfaction are significantly and negatively related to turnover. Graen & Ginsburgh (1977) demonstrated that role orientation, defined as perceived relevance of the job for workers' career, was significantly related to turnover.

McEvoy & Cascio (1987) conducted a meta-analysis, designed to estimate the direction and magnitude of the correlation between turnover and employee performance. The sample size-weighted mean correlation across 24 studies involving 7,717 individuals was found to be –0.28 suggesting that turnover is lower among good performers. Considerable unexplained variance in correlation coefficients across studies remained after correction for sampling error and attenuation. They found some support for three potential moderators : the type of turnover, the time span of measurement, and the level of unemployment.

Shore & Martin (1989) investigated the differential associations that job satisfaction and organizational commitment have with job performance and turnover intentions in a sample of bank tellers and hospital professionals. Their findings showed that organizational commitment was more strongly related than job satisfaction to turnover intentions for tellers but not for the professionals. Job satisfaction was related more strongly than organizational commitment to supervisory ratings of performance for both samples. Their findings suggest that specific job attitudes are more closely associated with task-related outcomes such as performance ratings, whereas global organizational attitudes are more closely associated with organizational outcomes like turnover intentions.

Borofsky and Watson (1994) examined early voluntary turnover and job performance of 78 private contract security officers. The analysis indicated a relationship between the number of days an individual remained on the job before quitting and scores on an inventory scale designed to assess the likelihood of early voluntary turnover. For a subject of this group, a suggestive relationship was also observed between supervisor's rating of job performance and scores on inventory scales designed to measure emotional maturity and work performance free from the disruptive use of substances and alcohol.

McBey (1996) examined individual job performance and reasons for turnover in a multivariate research study. Multiple, comprehensive measures of performance were used in the study including self-rated (subjective) and organizationally-assigned (objective) measures. Only the self-rated measures of performance were significant in their negative relationship with the actual turnover behaviour.

Russ & McNeilly (1995) explored the moderating impact of experience, gender, and performance on the relationships among job satisfaction dimensions, organizational commitment and turnover intentions. Their findings reveal that gender moderated the link between organizational commitment and turnover intentions. Experience and performance moderated the links between job satisfaction dimensions and organizational commitment. There also appeared to be a joint moderator effect of gender and experience on the strength of the relationship between turnover intentions and organizational commitment. Their results suggested the need for sales managers to manage adoptively, recognizing differences in different segments of the sale force.

Arthur (1994) investigated the effects of human resource systems on manufacturing performance and turnover. He found that the mills with commitment systems had higher productivity, lower scrap rates, and lower employees turnover than those with control system. Also, human resource system moderated the relationship between turnover and manufacturing performance.

Saks et al (1996) conducted a field study to examine the relationships between belief in the work ethic, job attitudes, intentions to quit and turnover in a sample of temporary service employees in a large Canadian theme park. When the turnover was measured as a function of the remaining employed with the organization until the end of the season, the turnover rate was 10% for high work ethic employees versus 33% for low work ethic employees. The results of a path analysis indicated that belief in the work ethic had an indirect effect on turnover. Specifically, belief in the work ethic was directly related to job satisfaction and organizational commitment and indirectly related to intentions to quit and turnover. Job satisfaction and intentions to quit were directly related to turnover.

Research studies indicate that the reward system may be an important moderator of performance – turnover relationship. For example, Johns (1989) found that better performers reported more turnover cognitions when rewards were not perceived as contingent upon performance (This relationship held for self-report performance and for rating of promotional potential, but not for the supervisory rating of performance). Similarly, Zenger (1992) reported that the turnover intentions were greatest among moderately high and extremely low performances in two firms with strong ties between pay and extreme performance. Harrison et al (1996) proposed and found evidence that when rewards are maximally contingent on performance, a strong relationship exists between performance and job satisfaction and thus high performers are less likely to quit.

Williams and Livingstone (1994) conducted a meta-analysis based on 55 studies and a total sample size of 15,138 to examine the critical relationship between performance and voluntary turnover. Results support the following conclusions : The negative relationship between performance and turnover was robust and unaffected by unemployment rates and the length of time between measurements of 2 variables. The negative performance-turnover relationship was stronger in organizations using performance-contingent rewards, and support was for a U-shaped relationship.

Oldham and Cummings (1996) examined the independent and joint contributions of employees creativity-relevant personal characteristics and three organizational characteristics (job complexity, supportive supervision, and controlling supervision) to indicators of creative performance (Patent disclosures written, contributions to an organization suggestion program, and supervisory ratings of creativity). Creative performance was highest when subjects had appropriate creativity relevant characteristics and worked in complex jobs with supportive and non-controlling supervision. The organizational context characteristics alone contributed independently to the performance and intentions to quit outcomes.

Jackofsky (1984) in her curvilinear hypothesis, proposed that performance directly influences perceptions of the chances of finding alternative employment. High performers are more likely than their lower performing coworkers to quit because their performance provides them more alternatives, whereas low performers are also more likely than other employees to leave because they are most likely to be involuntarily pushed out of the organization. In the middle performance range, adequate performers are less likely to quit because they are neither pushed out of the organization nor offered the high number of alternatives enjoyed by high performers.

Lance (1988) argued that Jackofsky's (1984) perspective would actually predict a positive relationship between job performance and voluntary turnover. High performers will have more alternatives available to them, whereas low performers will perceive fewer alternatives and thus will find it more difficult to leave, even if they want to or are informally encouraged to by the organization. Several studies have found evidence of a positive performance-turnover relationship, mostly among samples of scientists, faculty, and management employees (Jackofsky, 1984).

The foundation of much of the research in this area is March and Simon's (1958) ease and desirability of movement framework, which argues that an organization can continue only as long as the payments or inducements offered to employees are sufficient to elicit continued contributions, including participation in the organization. This framework suggests that the most important theoretical precursors of turnover are the ease and desirability of movement, the ease of movement primarily determined by the number of alternatives perceived and the desire to move primarily determined by job satisfaction. Desirability and ease of movement have subsequently been operationalized in the literature in terms of job satisfaction and perceived alternatives, respectively (Hom & Griffeth, 1995; Jackofsky et al, 1986). Lance (1988) held that arguments emphasizing the effects of performance on satisfaction and those emphasizing the effects of performance on alternatives represent competing perspectives.

Arguments focusing on performance effects on satisfaction and desirability of movement suggest a negative performance-turnover relationship. Because higher performers are likely to receive greater rewards from the organization, they are likely to have higher job satisfaction and less desire to leave (Dreher, 1982; Martin et al, 1981; Steers & Mowday, 1981). The majority of empirical results support a small negative relationship between performance and turnover in a wide variety of samples (Jackofsky, 1984). In addition, the meta-analytic evidence supports a moderate negative relationship between performance and turnover (Hom & Griffeth, 1995; McEvoy & Cascio, 1987; Williams & Livingstone, 1994).

The March & Simon (1958) turnover model suggests that voluntary employee separation is a function of perceived ease of movement and perceived desirability of movement. However, theoretical models of voluntary turnover often yield no simple prediction concerning the link with employees' performance (McEvoy & Cascio, 1987).

It has been suggested that turnover research is in a "fallow period" and in need of rejuvenation (O'Reilly, 1991). Indeed, several reviews and commentaries have indicated that most researchers have sought either to address methodological issues or to empirically validate the existing theories of withdrawal that focus on affect-induced quitting (Lee & Mitchell, 1994; O'Reilly, 1991). For these reasons, the turnover literature would benefit greatly from the introduction of alternative theoretical perspectives that take into account contextual variables surrounding the occurrence of quitting (Lee, 1996).

In this connection Aquino et al (1997) developed and tested a model clarifying the psychological processes by which felt deprivation instigates quitting. In their model, they posit that employees' outcome and supervisory satisfaction result from referent outcomes, justifications, and the likelihood of amelioration. These satisfaction facets are then related to turnover through withdrawal cognitions. Structural equation modeling was used to assess the fit of this model and alternatives. They found negative relationship between referent outcomes and outcome satisfaction, and positive relationship between interpersonal justification and supervisory satisfaction. The likelihood of amelioration also increased both the satisfaction facets.

Aquino et al (1997) research makes several theoretical and practical contributions to the literature. First, it supports Martin's (1981) argument that relative deprivation can increase turnover. Second, it fully describes and provides evidence for the psychological mechanisms by which felt deprivation emerges and activates quitting. Third, it outlines a model for future research in which the importance of perceived prospects for the amelioration of present circumstances, an overlooked turnover antecedent introduced by Mobley and Colleagues (1979), is recognized.

Thus, the relationship of employees' performance to turnover is a topic of growing interest, as evidenced by increasing attention to performance as a variable in model building (Allen & Griffeth, 2001; Aquino et al, 1997; Jackofsky, 1984; Rhodes & Doering, 1983; Steers & Mowday, 1981) and in empirical studies (Becker et al, 1996; Dreher, 1982; Jackofsky et al, 1986; Martin et al, 1981; McEvoy and Cascio, 1987; Sheridan, 1985; Stumpf & Hartman, 1984; Trevor et al, 1997; Williams and Livingstone, 1994; Sturman and Trevor, 2001; McElroy et al, 2001).

McEvoy & Cascio (1987) suggested three reasons for this increased interest. First, despite previous voluminous research on the correlates of turnover, the variance explained by the present models remains small (Steele & Ovalle, 1984). Therefore, scholars have made a few advances in understanding the phenomenon (Mobley, 1982). Second, we know less about the causes of turnover. In fact, there seems to be an emerging sense that little of what we have learned about turnover can be described as causal knowledge (Clegg, 1983) or can be of any practical use in helping managers to reduce turnover among valued employees (McEvoy & Cascio, 1985). The strongest relationship found to date is between intention to quit and turnover (Aquino et al, 1997).

Third, there has been an increasing interest in the consequences of turnover. Traditionally, investigators assumed that turnover is a negative phenomenon for organizations because valuable employees are lost, but current investigations have begun to question that assumption (Abelson & Baysinger, 1984; Dalton & Todor, 1982). Dalton et al (1981) found that much of the turnover among bank tellers in their study was actually beneficial because 42% of the leavers were poor performers. In a similar attempt, Hollenbeck and Williams (1986) found that just over half of the voluntary turnover among retail sales clerks was functional.

Research studies clearly indicate that turnover decreases as performance increases. McEvoy & Cascio (1987), Bycio et al (1990) and Williams & Livingstone (1994) have reported weighted uncorrected correlations of -.24, -.17, and -.16, respectively, in meta-analyses of voluntary performance and turnover. However, these and other authors have emphasized that such linear associations may not fully determine the nature of the relationship and that research should also address the potentially more informative issues of non-linearity and moderating effects (e.g., Jackofsky, 1984; McEvoy & Cascio, 1987; Schwab, 1991; Williams & Livingstone, 1994).

Thus, Trevor et al (1997) conducted a study that, for the first time, brings the curvilinear and moderator elements together into one framework. They investigated the relationship between job performance and voluntary employee turnover for 5,143 exempt employees in a single firm. Support was found for Jackofsky's (1984) curvilinear hypothesis, as turnover was higher for low and high performers than it was for average performers. Two potential moderators of the curvilinearity were examined in an attempt to explain conflicting results in the performance-turnover literature. Low salary growth and high promotions each produced a more pronounced curvilinear performance-turnover relationship. Most notably, salary growth effects on turnover were greatest for high performers, with high salary growth predicting rather low turnover for these employees, whereas low salary growth predicted extremely high turnover. Additionally, once salary growth was controlled, promotions positively predicted turnover, with poor performer turnover being most strongly affected.

More recently, Sturman and Trevor (2001) examined how the literatures of dynamic performance and the performance-turnover relationship inform each other. The nonrandom performance-turnover relationship suggests that dynamic performance studies may be biased by the elimination of participants who did not remain for the entire study period. They demonstrated that the performance slopes of those who leave an organization differ from the performance slopes of those who remain. Their finding suggests that studies of the performance-turnover relationship need to consider employee performance trends when predicting turnover. Replicating and extending the research of Harrison et al (1996), they found that performance changes from the previous month and performance trends measured over a longer time period explained variance in voluntary turnover beyond current performance. Finally, they showed that performance trends interacted with current performance in the prediction of voluntary turnover.

Reviews of the literature (e.g., Bluedorn, 1982; Jackofsky et al, 1986) found evidence for positive, negative, and no relationship conclusions. From a conceptual standpoint, some researchers (e.g., Cotton & Tuttle, 1986; Morrow et al, 1999; Vecchio & Norris, 1996; Williams & Livingstone, 1994; Dreher, 1982) have argued that performance and turnover ought to have a negative relationship, because higher performers are more likely to receive greater rewards and thus be less likely to want to leave. However, other researchers (e.g., Lance, 1988) have argued that performance and turnover might have a positive relationship, because higher performers are likely to have more alternative job opportunities and thus are more likely to be able to leave. Still others have argued that the performance-turnover relationship might be nonlinear (e.g., Jackofsky, 1984; Trevor et al, 1997) or nonexistent (e.g., Wright & Bonett, 1993).

Allen and Griffeth (2001) tested a more comprehensive model of the performance-turnover relationship that addresses at least three shortcomings of previous research. First, the model recognizes that performance may have simultaneous, and sometimes conflicting, effects on both the desire and the ability to leave an organization. Second, the model explicitly includes two important moderators of these relationships. Third, the model suggests that performance is a somewhat psychologically distal antecedent of turnover with effects that are mediated by other variables. Data consisted of organizational performance and turnover records and survey responses for 130 employees of a medical services organization. Results indicate that visibility and reward contingencies moderate performance relationships with alternatives and job satisfaction, respectively, and that performance may influence turnover through multiple mechanisms.

McElroy et al (2001) examined the differential effects of 3 types of turnover (voluntary, involuntary, and reduction-in-force) on measures of organizational subunit performance. Data were collected from 31 regional subunits of a national financial services company. Although each form of turnover exhibited adverse effects on subunit performance when examined separately, partial correlation results revealed greater and more pervasive adverse effects for reduction-in-force turnover (i.e. downsizing) in comparison to the effects of voluntary and involuntary turnover. The results confirm the negative effects of downsizing, suggesting the need to move beyond the traditional voluntary-involuntary classification scheme used in turnover research.

JOB SATISFACTION AND JOB PERFORMANCE

The study of the relationship between job satisfaction and job performance is one of the most venerable research traditions in industrial-organizational psychology. This relationship has been described as the "Holy Grail" of industrial psychologists (Landy, 1989). Indeed, interest in the link between workplace attitudes and productivity goes back at least as far as the Hawthorne studies (Roethlisberger & Dickson, 1939), and the topic continues to be written about to this day. The area has not lacked for qualitative (Brayfield & Crockett, 1955; Herzberg et al, 1957; Locke, 1970; Schwab & Cummings, 1970) or quantitative (Iaffaldano & Muchinsky, 1985; Petty et al, 1984; Judge et al, 2001) reviews.

Following the human relations movement, the most influential narrative review of the job satisfaction – job performance relationship was published by Brayfield and Crockett (1955). They reviewed studies relating job satisfaction to job performance as well as to a number of other behavioral outcomes (accidents, absence, and turnover). They concluded that there was not much of a relationship between job satisfaction and performance, labeling it as "minimal or no relationship". The Brayfield and Crockett review was limited by the very small number of published studies available for review at that time (only nine studies were reviewed that reported a correlation between individual job satisfaction and job performance) and the general subjectivity of qualitative reviews. In spite of these shortcomings, Brayfield and Crockett's article was perhaps the most frequently cited review in the area of research prior to 1985.

Since the Brayfield and Crockett (1955) review, several other influential narrative reviews have been published. Herzberg et al (1957) presented an extensive review on this topic. Vroom (1964) in his book, brings the research in this category up-to-date and concludes that job satisfaction determines performance. He found a median correlation of 0.14, with a range of 0.86 to –0.31. He also examined the relationship between satisfaction and various other aspects of job behaviour such as turnover, absenteeism, accidents and job performance. These reviews differed greatly in their orientation and, to some degree, in the optimism they expressed regarding the satisfaction-performance relationship, with Herzberg et al (1957) being the most optimistic. Findings of Vroom (1964) and Locke (1976) showed no strong relationship between job satisfaction and job performance. However, Khaleque (1979) found a significant positive correlation between job satisfaction and performance. Haque (1991) and Hossain (1995) also found significant positive correlation between job satisfaction and performance.

Keaveney and Nelson (1993) tested a complex model of the interrelationship among numerous attitudes (intrinsic motivation orientation, role conflict, role ambiguity, psychological withdrawal) and found a job satisfaction – job performance path coefficient of .12 (ns) in a relatively saturated model involving these attitudes; a simpler model provided a much stronger (.29) but still nonsignificant coefficient.

Shore and Martin (1989) found that regressing supervisory ratings of job performance on job satisfaction and organizational commitment, job satisfaction explained more incremental variance in the performance of professionals and clerical workers than did commitment.

Podsakoff and Williams (1986) observed that satisfied workers may not necessarily be the highest producers. They found that the general satisfaction-job performance relationship was somewhat stronger in studies in which rewards were linked to performance (mean r=.27) than in studies where there was no performance-pay contingency (mean r=.17). So, they concluded that there are many possible mediating factors, the most important of which seems to be the reward.

Aspects of work environment may also influence the satisfaction-performance relationship. Bhagat (1982) revealed that intense time and performance pressures produced a situation where performance and job satisfaction were essentially unrelated. However, in the absence of these pressures, a strong positive relationship emerged between satisfaction and performance. Two of the more constant findings in this research are that people who are relatively satisfied with their jobs, will stay in them longer, i.e. lower turnover, and be less absent (Locke, 1976; Jewell & Segall, 1990).

Myriad other moderators of the satisfaction-performance have been proposed and/or tested, including job complexity or intrinsic job characteristics (Baird, 1976), self-esteem (Korman, 1970), attributions and organizational tenure (Norris & Niebuhr, 1984), cognitive ability (Varca & James-Valutis, 1993), need for achievement (Steers, 1975), career stage (Stumpf & Rabinowitz, 1981), pressure for performance (Ewen, 1973), job fit (Carlson, 1969), occupational group (Doll & Gunderson, 1969), dyadic duration (Mossholder et al, 1994), similarity in problem-solving styles (Goldsmith et al, 1989), perceived appropriateness of supervisory task allocation decisions (Jabri, 1992), affective disposition (Hochwarter et al, 1999), and situational constraints (Herman, 1973).

Most studies that include job satisfaction and job performance treat them as separate variables that have no direct relationship to each other. For example, Greenberger et al (1989) investigated the causal relationship between personal control and job satisfaction, and between personal control and job performance, but did not investigate the relationship between job satisfaction and job performance. They might ignore the satisfaction-performance relationship, while including the two constructs in their study, for different reasons. For example, they might be convinced there is no relationship between job satisfaction and job performance, and/or they might believe that investigating the relationship between the constructs is beyond the scope of their study.

Organ (1988) suggested that the failure to find a relationship between job satisfaction and performance is due to the narrow means often used to define job performance. Typically, researchers have equated job performance with performance of specific job tasks. However, some researchers (Borman & Motowidlo, 1993) have broadened the performance domain to include citizenship behaviors.

Similarly, Ostroff (1992) noted that one possible reason that the satisfaction-performance relationship has not been substantiated is that researchers have considered the relationship solely at the individual level of analysis. He investigated the relationship between satisfaction, attitudes, and performance at the organizational level of analysis. Support was found for links between satisfaction and organizational performance. He found significant correlations between average teacher job satisfaction in a school district and numerous indicators of school district effectiveness. In several other studies, all of which were completed in the same educational context, Ostroff and colleagues have revealed reliable relations between job satisfaction and performance at the organizational level (Ostroff, 1993; Ostroff & Schmitt, 1993). Harter and Creglow

(1998) linked overall satisfaction to various indicators (customer satisfaction, profitability, productivity, turnover) of the performance of a variety of business units.

In the past, there have been two meta-analyses of the job satisfaction-job performance relationship. Petty et al (1984) provided a limited meta-analysis of the job satisfaction-job performance relationship. They confined their analysis to 16 studies that were published in five journals from 1964 to 1983 and these included a measure of overall job satisfaction. Correcting the correlations for unreliability in job satisfaction and job performance, Petty et al. reported a mean corrected correlation of .31 between the constructs. In interpreting their results, Petty et al (1984) concluded, "The results of the present study indicate that the relationship between individual, overall job satisfaction and individual job performance is stronger and more consistent than that reported in previous reviews."

At about the same time as the Petty et al (1984) review, Iaffaldano and Muchinsky (1985) conducted a more comprehensive meta-analysis of the job satisfaction-job performance literature. Meta-analyzing 217 correlations from 74 studies, they found a substantial range in satisfaction-performance correlations across the job satisfaction facets, ranging from a mean "true score" correlation of .06 for pay satisfaction to .29 for overall job satisfaction. For their primary analysis, Iaffaldano and Muchinsky (1985) averaged the facet-performance correlations and reported on average true score correlation of .17 between job satisfaction and job performance. In discussing their findings, they only made reference to the .17 correlation, concluding that job satisfaction and job performance were "only slightly related to each other."

Iaffaldano and Muchinsky (1985) also examined nine moderators of the satisfaction-performance relationship. With one exception (white-collar vs. blue-collar occupational type), the moderators pertained to the measures of job satisfaction (e.g., composite of satisfaction, global, unknown-unspecified) and job performance (e.g., quality vs. quantity, objective vs. subjective). The moderator analysis was not particularly successful – none of the moderators correlated .20 or greater with the satisfaction-performance correlation. They concluded that the moderators were "of little consequence."

Because Iaffaldano and Muchinsky (1985) concluded that there was no appreciable relationship between job satisfaction and job performance, researchers have accepted this conclusion, as evidenced by the following statements : "The seminal research on job satisfaction and job performance suggests that there exists only a modest correlation between these two constructs" (Cote, 1999); "It is accepted among most researchers that there is not a substantial relationship between job satisfaction and productivity" (Judge et al, 1995); "Much evidence indicates that individual job satisfaction generally is not significantly related to individual task performance" (Brief, 1998); "The magnitude of correlation between job performance and job satisfaction is unexpectedly low" (Spector, 1997); "modest... at best" (Katzell et al, 1992); "disappointing" (Wiley, 1996); "negligible" (Weiss & Cropanzano, 1996) and "bordering on the trivial" (Landy, 1989).

Thus, the bulk of evidence shows the correlation between satisfaction and performance to be relatively low (Brayfield & Crockett, 1955; Iaffaldano & Muchinsky, 1985; Locke, 1976; Vroom, 1964). A variety of reasons, such as measurement problems (Fisher, 1980), research design characteristics (Iaffaldano & Muchinsky, 1985), the moderating effects of job characteristics (Ivancevich, 1978), constraints on performance (Bhagat, 1982; Herman, 1973), personality characteristics (Steers, 1975), and rewards (Porter & Lawler, 1968; Schwab & Cumming, 1970), have been offered to explain the small degree of correlation with the exception of moderating effects of rewards, but the satisfaction-performance research has still failed to produce strong and unambiguous findings.

Ellingson et al (1998) reported an uncorrected satisfaction-performance correlation of .30. Similarly, Judge et al (2001) conducted a meta-analysis on 312 samples with a combined N of 54,417. The mean true correlation between overall job satisfaction and job performance was estimated to be .30. This average uncorrected correlation is higher because Iaffaldano and Muchinsky (1985) analyzed correlations at the single satisfaction facet level. This lack of correspondence in terms of generality-using a specific attitude to predict a general behavior - should result in a lower correlation (Wanous et al, 1989).

Hossain and Islam (1999) investigated the overall quality of working life (QWL) and job satisfaction, and performance of the government hospital nurses in Bangladesh. QWL refers to a relationship between the worker and work environment. A total number of 63 nurses were selected from three government hospitals on a stratified random sampling basis. The results reveal that there was significant positive correlation between QWL and job satisfaction. A significant positive correlation was also found between QWL and performance and, job satisfaction and performance. QWL had the highest contribution to performance. Perceptions of QWL and job satisfaction were significantly higher among the respondents in small organisations than in large organisations. Morning shift nurses perceived higher QWL and job satisfaction than the night shift nurses. Night shift nurses were suffering from more problems than the nurses of other shifts.

Dolke (2000) examined the effects of various job attitudes on employees' job behaviour and mental health. The data were collected on a sample of 122 supervisors working in 11 textile mills in Mumbai. The semi-structured interview schedule was used to collect the data. The results showed that job attitudes significantly affected work behaviour and mental health. Positive job attitudes resulted in better performance, lower employee turnover, lower absenteeism, better feelings towards job and gave added confidence to the supervisors. Negative job attitudes, on the other hand, adversely affected interpersonal relations with superiors and opinion towards profession. Negative job attitudes also induced a sense of insecurity, psychosomatic and tension symptoms, and resulted in low motivation, lowered self-esteem, job dissatisfaction, high-job related tension, and increased smoking and drinking.

Steele-Johnson et al (2000) investigated the joint effects of goal orientation and task demands on motivation, affect, and performance, in two studies. In study 1 (N=199), task difficulty was found to moderate the effect of goal orientation on performance and affect (i.e., satisfaction with performance). In study 2 (N=189), task consistency was found to moderate the effect of goal orientation on self-efficacy and intrinsic motivation.

Janssen (2001) studied fairness perceptions as a moderator in the curvilinear relationships between job demands, and job performance and job dissatisfaction. Using an equity theory framework, the author hypothesized that perceptions of effort-reward fairness moderate these inverted U-shaped demand-response relationships. A sample of 99 low-level and mid-level management employees (mean age 45.33 yrs) from a Dutch industrial organization filled out questionnaires. In support of this hypothesis, survey results demonstrate that managers who perceive effort-reward fairness perform better and feel more satisfied in response to intermediate levels of job demands than managers who perceive "under reward unfairness."

Grant et al (2001) examined the satisfaction with territory design from the perspective of the salesperson. They developed a conceptual model and hypotheses linking the satisfaction with territory design with role ambiguity, intrinsic motivation, job satisfaction, and performance. Role conflict, met expectations, organizational commitment, and intention to leave are also included in the model. Survey results from 148 salespeople (mean age 34 yrs; 87% male) from 27 different companies provide strong support for 19 of the 21 hypotheses examined. Findings offer significant insights concerning the role of territory design satisfaction in face-to-face selling and its consequences.

Pettijohn et al (2001) investigated the relationship between performance appraisal characteristics and salesperson job satisfaction. Using data from 115 salespeople, they indicated that when appraisals provide clear criteria, the criteria meet with the salesperson's approval, and when the appraisals are perceived as fair and used in determining rewards, salesperson's job satisfaction increases. These results support the previous findings that the critical determinants of appraisal effectiveness are not criteria-driven but rather are largely determined by factors that managers can influence.

Nagy (2002) investigated the use of a single-item approach measuring facet satisfaction. Participants consisted of 207 employees from a variety of organizations who completed a job satisfaction survey containing the Job Descriptive Index (JDI) as well as a single-item which also measured each of the five JDI facets. Results indicated that the single-item facet measure was significantly correlated with each of the JDI facets (correlations ranged from .60 to .72). Results also indicated that the single-item approach compared favourably to the JDI and in some cases accounted for incremental variance in self-reported job performance and intentions to turnover.

SELF-EFFICACY AND JOB PERFORMANCE

Two decades of empirical research have generated a great number of studies that demonstrated the positive relationship between self-efficacy and different motivational and behavioral outcomes in clinical (e.g., Bandura et al, 1980), educational (e.g., Lent et al, 1994; Schunk, 1995), and organizational settings (e.g., Bandura, 1988; Wood & Bandura, 1989). Regarding the relationship between self-efficacy and performance in organizational settings, in the initial years of self-efficacy research, only a few studies were conducted. They revealed that self-efficacy was related to job search (Ellis & Taylor, 1983), insurance sales (Barling & Beattie, 1983) and research productivity of university faculty members (Taylor et al, 1984).

Empirical research has demonstrated that self-efficacy is related to a number of other work-performance measures such as adaptability to advanced technology (Hill et al, 1987), coping with career-related events (Stumpf et al, 1987), managerial idea generating (Gist, 1989), managerial performance (Wood et al, 1990), skill acquisition (Mitchell et al, 1994), newcomer adjustment to an organizational setting (Saks, 1995), and naval performance at sea (Eden & Zuk, 1995).

A person's self-efficacy expectation concerning the ability to successfully perform a given task is a reliable predictor of whether a person will attempt the task, how much effort he or she will spend and how much the person will persevere in pursuing the task in the face of unforeseen difficulties. (Bandura, 1989). He demonstrated that perceived self-efficacy enhances performance through its effects on cognitive, affective or motivational intervening processes. The subjects having high perceived confidence in being able to perform on specific tasks indeed did well on those tasks and vice-versa (Schunk & Gunn, 1986). It will also be observed that as the self-efficacy perception for any task improved, so did the performance on the related measure.

Self-efficacy, a significant component in Bandura's social cognitive theory, has enormous effects on one's effort, interest, persistence and performance. Researchers have reported strong relationship between self-efficacy and performance of a specific task (Taylor et al, 1984; Lent et al, 1987). It is evident from the literature that individual self-efficacy of performing a task is positively related to individual performance. Numerous organizational behaviour studies focus on improving self-efficacy in order to improve both individual and organizational performance.

Gist and Mitchell (1992) proposed a model to explain self-efficacy-performance relationship. The model provides a simplified display of the process of self-efficacy formation and its relation with performance. Overall, this model implies that people directly and indirectly evaluate their experience and arrive at judgements about the extent of their abilities to perform a specific task. The model proposes that four kinds of experience influence an individual's self-efficacy through his/her cognitive evaluation, which, in turn, affects the individual's performance. Individual performance is also found to be related to satisfaction.

Several studies have suggested that efficacy beliefs facilitate integration and effective use of complex information. Bandura & Jourden (1991), Bandura & Wood (1989), and Wood & Bandura (1989) found that individuals with high (vs. low) self-efficacy performed significantly better in management simulations requiring complex information integration and learning of nonlinear probabilities and contingencies. Cervone et al (1991) commented that individuals with high self-efficacy "learn more from feedback, respond more adaptively to the decision environment, and, over time, are better able to translate their learning into improved performance."

Wood & Bandura (1989) observed that perceived self-efficacy had both a direct effect on organizational performance and an indirect effect through its influence on analytic strategies. Self-efficacy is highly relevant in settings that involve physical performance. Feelings of self-efficacy can lead to better performance, independently of the person's ability. Gould and Weiss (1981) also found that people high in self-efficacy are able to last longer than low-efficacy individuals in exercise involving physical endurance. Bandura and his colleagues (1988) were able to show that physical performance lasts longer because high self-efficacy stimulates the body to produce endogenous options, which function as natural painkillers.

A number of studies have been carried out by researches to examine the effect of self-efficacy on human performance. McDonald and Siegall (1992) investigated the impact of self-efficacy on the performance and attitudes of telecommunications field service technicians whose jobs had undergone a major technological change. It was concluded that technological self-efficacy was positively correlated with satisfaction, commitment, work quality and quantity. Similarly, Mathieu and Button (1992) observed significant impact of self-efficacy beliefs on personal goals and performance over time.

Locke et al (1984) examined the effect of self-efficacy, goals, and task strategies on goal choice and task performance. They manipulated self-efficacy and task strategies through training. They found that ability, past performance, and self-efficacy were the major predictors of goal choice. Ability, self-efficacy, goals, and task strategies were all related to task performance. Self-efficacy was more strongly related to past performance than to future performance but remained a significant predictor of future performance even when past performance was controlled. Self-efficacy ratings for moderate to difficult levels of performance were the best predictors of future performance.

Mitchell et al (1994) also investigated the effect of self-efficacy on performance and found that self-efficacy is a better predictor of performance than expected score or goals. Gage and Polatajko (1994) also concluded that assessment and monitoring of perceived self-efficacy will result in the improved occupational performance.

Orpen (1995) examined the relationship between self-efficacy beliefs and job performance among black managers in South Africa. A significant positive correlation was obtained between self-efficacy beliefs and self-rating of performance. The findings confirmed the results of studies in western industrialized countries and suggested that among these Black supervisors encouraging self-efficacy beliefs had beneficial consequences for job performance.

Sadri and Robertson (1993) presented a comprehensive review of studies on relationship between self-efficacy and work-related behaviours. The results of meta-analyses supported the view that self-efficacy is related to performance and they also found that self-efficacy performance links appeared weaker in field studies than in laboratory situations.

In a meta-analysis Stajkovic and Luthans (1997) observed a high significant relationship between self-efficacy and performance in organizational settings. So, a stream of research studies has established a fairly clear association between self-efficacy and work-related performance. Similarly, they also conducted another meta-analysis in 1998 to examine the relationship between self-efficacy and work-related performance. They analyzed the results of 114 studies, and 21,616 subjects. The results of the primary meta-analysis indicated a significant weighted average correlation between self-efficacy and work-related performance $G(r_{+})=.38$, and a significant within-group heterogeneity of individual correlations. The meta-analytically-derived average correlation of .38 also seems to indicate that self-efficacy may be a better predictor of work-related performance than much of the personality-trait-based constructs commonly-used in organizational research (see Adler & Weiss, 1988; George, 1992; Ghiselli, 1971; Weiss & Adler, 1984). When converted to the commonly used affect size estimate used in meta-analysis, the transformed value represents a 28 percent increase in performance due to self-efficacy.

The relationship between self-efficacy and performance is cyclic in nature, performance affects self-efficacy, which, in turn, affects performance, and so on. Lindsley et al (1995) explored the possibility of efficacy performance spirals in individual groups, and organizations spirals, which were deviation amplifying loops in which the positive, cyclic relationship between perceived efficacy and performance builds upon itself. The study specifies the notion of upward (overconfidence) and downward (lack of confidence) spirals and consider how they occur, continue, and stop, as well as their consequences, using multiple levels of analysis. Consideration is given to compositional and cross level effects by proposing 5 factors (task inter-dependence, task uncertainty and complexity, size, social-identity and inclusion) that moderate the relationship between spirals at different levels of analysis.

Researchers have documented a strong linkage between high self-efficacy expectations and success in widely varied physical and mental tasks, anxiety reduction, addiction control, pain tolerance, illness recovery, and avoidance of sea sickness in naval cadets (Eden & Zuk, 1995; Gecas, 1989; Stevens et al, 1993). Also, those with high self-efficacy have the tendency to remain calm in a stressful situation (Bandura et al, 1985). In other words, there is considerable evidence that those employees with high self-efficacy tend to persevere and end up doing a good job without suffering stress or burnout.

Oppositely, those with low self-efficacy expectations tend to have low success rates. Chronically low self-efficacy is associated with a conditional called learned helplessness, the severly debilitating belief that one has no control over ones environment (Gecas, 1989; Martinko & Gardner, 1982).

Schaubroeck and Merritt (1997) reviewed the evidence from laboratory research supporting the role of self-efficacy in how people respond to control and demands. Specifically, they examined the three-way interaction between job demands, control, and self-efficacy. Control perceptions capture an individual's appraisal of an objective situation (Ganster, 1989), whereas self-efficacy influences the individual's evaluation of his or her personal ability to exercise control (Wood & Bandura, 1989). It was suggested that it is mostly the workers with high confidence in their abilities whose coping is facilitated by having a high level of control.

On similar lines recently, Schaubroeck et al (2000) examined how cultural differences and efficacy perceptions influence the role of job control in coping with job demands. Perceiving higher control mitigated the effects of demands on psychological health symptoms and turnover intentions only among American bank tellers, reporting high job self-efficacy. Among American tellers reporting low job self-efficacy, perceived control exacerbated the effects of demands. However, in a matched Hong Kong sample, collective efficacy interacted in the same way with control and demands as job self-efficacy had in the American sample. These differences appear to be explained by the individual attributes of idiocentrism and allocentrism that are linked to the societal norms of individualism and collectivism, respectively.

Gardner and Pierce (1998) examined the intervening role of organization-based self-esteem in the relationship between generalized self-efficacy and explored two outcomes, employee's job performance and job-related affect (job satisfaction). Self-report data were collected from 145 professional employees on generalized self-efficacy, organization-based self-esteem and satisfaction and commitment, and 8 months later, performance-rating data were collected from the supervisor-manager. Subjects also completed 3 measures of employee job related affect. Results show that organization-based self-esteem emerged as a stronger predictor and it acted as a mediator in the relationship between generalized self-efficacy and employee responses.

Comparing the validity of self-efficacy with self-esteem for predicting performance, Mone et al (1996) conducted a study on 215 undergraduate subjects. It was observed that across three performance trials, self-efficacy had greater predictive validity than self-esteem in predicting performance.

Applications in organizational literature have demonstrated consistently that self-efficacy positively predicts personal goals, task learning, direction and persistence of effort, task performance levels and attributions made for performance levels (e.g. Bandura, 1997; Button et al, 1996; Gist, 1987; Locke & Latham, 1990).

Mone (1994) examined a model of self-efficacy, self-esteem, and goals in relation to these variables in a downsizing organization. As in other studies (e.g., Locke et al, 1984; Wood & Locke, 1987), Mone found that self-efficacy significantly predicted goals; however, extending past work, he found that in a downsizing organization, self-efficacy was positively related to the intention to leave, suggesting that in such situations, those who consider themselves more capable may seek and be able to find work elsewhere.

In addition he found that self-efficacy was inversely related to job satisfaction and organizational commitment suggesting that in a downsizing organization, higher self-confidence and performance are not necessarily met with the commensurate rewards and job security that help create job satisfaction and affective commitment.

It is generally accepted that self-efficacy and performance are positively related, but questions have arisen over the validity of this conclusion (Hawkins, 1992; Vancouver et al, 2001; Powers, 1973, 1991). Stone (1994) found that inducing mild negative expectations improved performance as compared to those given positive expectation information. He found that high self-efficacy led to overconfidence in one's abilities. Instead of high-self-efficacy individuals contributing more of their resources toward the task, they contributed less. These participants were both less attentive and effortful than were their low-self-efficacy counterparts. Bandura and Jourden (1991) found similar results. Using normative feedback, these authors induced high self-efficacy in a group of participants. In reviewing the effects of this manipulation on performance, they found that these participants' performance did not increase. In fact, over time, the higher self-efficacy contributed to decrements in performance. Bandura and Jourden (1991) explained self-efficacy's negative effect by concluding, "complacent self-assurance creates little incentive to expend the increased effort needed to attain high levels of performance." In a creative task, Podsakoff and Farh (1989) found that a negative normative feedback, a common efficacy-manipulation, led to better performance than positive feedback. On a cognitively complex task, Cervone and Wood (1995) found negative correlations between self-efficacy and subsequent performance, which they explained as individuals being too confident in their abilities. Similarly, Waldersee and Luthans (1994) found that those in the positive-feedback group had poorer performance on a highly routine work task than individuals in the control or corrective (i.e., negative) feedback groups.

Vancouver et al (2001) questioned the common interpretation of the positive correlation among self-efficacy, personal goals, and performance. Using self-efficacy theory (Bandura, 1977), it was predicted that cross-sectional correlational results were a function of past performance's influence on self-efficacy, and using control theory (Powers,

1973), it was predicted that self-efficacy could negatively influence subsequent performance. These predictions were supported with 56 undergraduate participants, using a with-in-person procedure. Personal goals were also positively influenced by self-efficacy and performance, but negatively related to subsequent performance. A 2nd study involving 185 undergraduates found that manipulated goal level positively predicted performance and self-efficacy positively predicted performance in the difficult-goal condition.

Vancouver et al (2002) examined the negative effect of self-efficacy on performance. They presented 2 studies to (a) confirm the causal role of self-efficacy and (b) substantiate the explanation. In study 1, self-efficacy was manipulated for 43 of 87 undergraduates on an analytic game. The manipulation was negatively related to performance on the next trial. In study 2, 104 undergraduates played the analytic game and reported self-efficacy between each game and confidence in the degree to which they had assessed previous feedback. As expected, self-efficacy led to overconfidence and hence increased the likelihood of committing logic errors during the game.

Shea and Howell (2000) examined the pattern of relationships between self-efficacy and performance in an experiment involving 148 students (with mean age of 27 yrs.) who worked on a manufacturing task over 4 trials. Task feedback and task experience, 2 variables that may influence the occurrence of efficacy-performance spirals, were also investigated. The experimental task involved the manufacture of a real electrical wiring harness, modified so that individuals with no experience in this type of work would be able to produce the harness within 15 minutes. Results indicated strong support for a significant relationship between self-efficacy and performance over time. However, the pattern of changes in self-efficacy and performance from trial-to-trial contained self-corrections, suggesting that the efficacy-performance relationship does not necessarily proceed in a monotonic, deviation-amplifying spiral. Task feedback and task experience affected the occurrence of self-corrections in the pattern of changes in self-efficacy and performance over time. Implications are drawn about the dynamic nature of self-efficacy.

Endler et al (2001) investigated the relationship between General self-efficacy and control in relation to anxiety and cognitive performance. The investigation employed a general measure of self-efficacy, a measure of perceived control, and items relating to expectation and evaluation (pre and post). The purpose of the study was to determine whether general self-efficacy or perceived-control best predicted the criterion variables of state anxiety and performance on a stressful cognitive task under conditions of high vs low control, using a sample of 80 college students. These relationships were tested under the experimental conditions of high and low objective control. Results show that general self-efficacy, relative to perceived control is a better predictor of state anxiety in the high and low control conditions but neither predicts actual performance. Participants' expectations of task difficulty, their own performance and their performance relative to the performance of others taken before the task were compared with their evaluations of difficulty and performance after completing the task. Participants indicated that the task was easier than anticipated, but rated their own performance more poorly after completion of the task.

Chen et al (2001) examined meta-analytically whether self-efficacy mediates the cognitive ability-performance and conscientiousness-performance relationships, and whether task complexity moderates the extent to which self-efficacy mediates these relationships. Results indicated that cognitive ability and conscientiousness positively relate to self-efficacy, but that the magnitude of these relationships varies with task complexity. Furthermore, results showed that self-efficacy mediates the relationships of cognitive ability and conscientiousness with performance on simple tasks, but not on complex tasks.

Renn and Fedor (2001) conducted a field study to examine the relationships among a set of feedback-seeking, social cognitive, and goal-setting constructs and the work performance of 136 sales and customer-service representatives. As they hypothesized, feedback-seeking and self-efficacy related to two dimensions of work performance (i.e., work quantity and work quality) through feedback-based goals. In addition, self-efficacy and feedback seeking mediated the relationship between two individual differences (viz., personal-control perceptions and external feedback propensity) and both dimensions of work performance. The findings extend research on work performance by underscoring the importance of incorporating feedback into work-related improvement goals when investigating the relationship between feedback seeking and work performance. The findings also provide insight into the motivational processes underlying the relationship among personal control perceptions, external feedback propensity, and work performance.

Brown et al (2001) assessed previously unexplored processes by which information seeking and self-efficacy contribute to self-regulatory effectiveness in industrial selling. They assessed the synergistic interaction of inquiry and monitoring with respect to role clarity and tested whether this interaction was further moderated by self-efficacy. Results indicated that the role-clarifying effects of feedback inquiry and monitoring were contingent rather than independent. Role clarity increased as the combination of inquiry and monitoring increased. Furthermore, these joint effects were moderated by self-efficacy, such that high-self-efficacy employees were able to effectively use the combination of inquiry and monitoring to clarify role expectations, whereas low-self-efficacy employees could not.

Mangos and Steele-Johnson (2001) examined the role of subjective task complexity in goal-orientation effects on self-efficacy and performance on a computerized simulation of a class-scheduling task (N=138). Results indicated that goal-orientation effects on performance were mediated by subjective task complexity. In addition, the results revealed that subjective task complexity was related to self-efficacy but not cognitive ability. Moreover, subjective task complexity effects on performance were mediated by self-efficacy, and goal-orientation effects on self-efficacy were mediated by subjective task complexity.

Bell and Kozlowski (2002) examined the direct relationship of goal orientation – and the interaction of goal orientation and cognitive ability – with self-efficacy, performance, and knowledge in a learning context. The authors argue that whether a particular type of goal orientation is adaptive or not adaptive depends on individuals' cognitive ability. Consistent with previous research, learning orientation was positively related to self-efficacy, performance, and knowledge, whereas performance orientation was negatively related to performance only. As expected, learning orientation was generally adaptive for high-ability individuals but had no effect for low-ability individuals. In contrast, the effects of performance orientation were contingent on both individual's level of cognitive ability and the outcome examined.

JOB SATISFACTION AND TURNOVER INTENTIONS

Empirical work over the years has clearly established the significant role of job satisfaction in predicting turnover. Carsten and Spector (1987), in a meta-analysis of 47 studies, estimated a corrected correlation between job satisfaction and turnover of -.26. They found that alternative employment opportunities moderated the relationship between job satisfaction and turnover.

Weitz (1952) argued that job dissatisfaction would be more predictive of turnover if it was considered in the light of an individual's predisposition to be satisfied with everyday life events. He suggested that "some individuals generally gripe more than others" and that such individuals when dissatisfied with their jobs, are less likely to quit than are those more positively disposed toward life.

Mobley's (1977) psychological process model of turnover provides some support for Weitz's (1952) hypothesis. Mobley argued that job dissatisfaction is translated into thoughts of quitting, evaluation of alternatives, and ultimately, turnover because quitting is expected to result in a more satisfying job. However, those more negatively disposed toward life may have no such expectation. For them, job dissatisfaction simply may be another dissatisfying element in an already dissatisfying world. This is supported by research suggesting that job satisfaction may derive from genetic or early childhood influences (Arvey et al, 1989; Staw et al, 1986). Thus, for these individuals, job dissatisfaction and quitting may seem to have little to do with each other. On the other hand, job dissatisfaction is much more salient and generates more tension for generally happy individuals, and changing jobs may appear to be a viable means of correcting one of the few dissatisfying elements in their lives.

Similarly, Judge (1993) conducted a study in which it was hypothesized that affective disposition moderates the relationship between job satisfaction and voluntary turnover. Their findings reveal that the more positive the disposition of the individual, the stronger the relationship that was observed between job dissatisfaction and turnover. Furthermore, individuals dissatisfied with their jobs but positively disposed to life in general were the individuals most likely to quit.

One of the most consistent findings about job satisfaction is that it correlates negatively with turnover (Mowday et al, 1982). Hulin (1966) compared clerical workers, who subsequently quit, to a matched sample of those who did not quit. Job-satisfaction measures were obtained from both groups prior to the resignation of those who quited. Turnover was clearly related (negatively) to job satisfaction. In a follow-up study, Hulin (1968) made changes in the jobs to correct some of the dissatisfying factors mentioned by those who quit. These changes led to significant decreases in turnover. Lee & Mowday (1987) and Tett & Meyer (1993) observed a moderate relationship between these two variables. They also concluded that high job satisfaction leads to lower turnover, while low satisfaction leads to higher turnover.

The consistency of the negative relationship between job satisfaction and turnover has led investigators to look more closely at other factors that might be related to issues of turnover and job satisfaction. Jackofsky and Peters (1983) argued that dissatisfaction with the job should only lead to turnover when employees believed that alternative employment is available to them. This position followed directly from the classic work of March and Simons (1958), which posited that dissatisfaction leads to search for alternative jobs and that search increases the likelihood that alternatives will be found. Jackofsky and Peters (1983) simply argued that, if this were true, only those who believe alternative jobs exist which they are likely to obtain will quit when they are dissatisfied.

Spencer and Steers (1981) found a strong negative relationship between job satisfaction and turnover only for hospital employees who were relatively low performers. These authors felt that high-performing employees who became dissatisfied were encouraged to stay by receiving whatever inducements could be provided to change their feelings. Low performers, on the other hand, received no such encouragement; therefore, job satisfaction was more likely to be related to quitting for them than for the high performers.

Hellman (1997) conducted a meta-analysis to determine the generalizability of the relationship between job satisfaction and intent to leave. The results were consistent with the following hypothesis : the relationship between job satisfaction and intent to leave was significantly different from zero and consistently negative.

Lum et al (1998) assessed both the direct and indirect impact of certain pay policies upon the turnover intentions of 361 predominantly female pediatric nurses. The two major questions addressed were (1) What was the relative impact of job satisfaction, pay satisfaction, and organizational commitment upon the turnover intentions of pediatric nurses eligible for these pay policies ? and (2) What model accurately portrays the relationship among these 3 independent variables and turnover intentions ? The results suggest that job satisfaction has only an indirect influence on the intention to quit, whereas organizational commitment has the strongest and most direct impact. A further finding that pay satisfaction has both direct and indirect effects on turnover intent was consistent with administrators' assumptions underlying the pay policies.

Hom and Kinicki (2001) generalized a leading portrayal of how job dissatisfaction progresses into turnover (Hom & Griffeth, 1991) and more rigorously tested this model using structural equations modeling and survival analysis. The authors further integrated job avoidance, interrole conflict, and employment conditions into this framework. Using a national survey of 438 retail store personnel, the authors found that interrole conflict and job avoidance influence turnover indirectly, as the Hom-Griffeth (1991) model specifies, and that unemployment rates directly affect turnover.

In a similar manner, Lui et al (2001) examined the effect of interrole conflicts on job satisfaction and the propensity to leave. Data were collected from a sample of 251 professional accountants employed in Hong Kong firms. Results from hierarchical regression analyses revealed that interrole conflict was associated with low job satisfaction and the high propensity to leave. In addition, it was found that professional commitment moderated the relationship between interrole conflict and the propensity to leave.

Trevor (2001) emphasized that both general job availability and individual attributes determine actual ease of movement in the job market. A voluntary turnover model that combines aspects of signaling and human capital perspectives with approaches emphasizing job satisfaction and general job availability was proposed. Longitudinal data on 5,506 individuals (aged 27-34 yrs) were analyzed via survival analysis with time-dependent covariates and repeated turnover events. Most notably, the effects of job satisfaction and unemployment rate on voluntary turnover were moderated by education, cognitive ability, and occupation-specific training.

Schwepker (2001) examined ethical climate's relationship to job satisfaction, organizational commitment, and turnover intention among salespeople. 152 salespeople participated. Although salespeople are believed to be physically, psychologically, and socially separated from the organization, results suggest that the organization's ethical climate nevertheless influences them. Results suggest that salespeople's perceptions of a positive ethical climate are positively associated with their job satisfaction and organizational commitment.

Blau et al (2001) presents initial evidence for differentiating two different facets of benefit satisfaction-basic and career enrichment. Basic benefit satisfaction exhibited stronger relationships to subsequent general benefit satisfaction, organizational withdrawal intent, and turnover behavior, while career enrichment benefit satisfaction exhibited a stronger relationship to subsequent affective organizational commitment.

Harrington et al (2001) examined the predictors of intentions to leave a job in a military setting. They studied a stratified random sample of 139 Air Force Family Advocacy Program workers. Respondents were more likely to intend to leave if they were emotionally exhausted, had lower levels of intrinsic job satisfaction, and were dissatisfied with their salary and promotion opportunities.

Honda-Howard & Homma (2001) analyzed 177 currently full-time employed individuals in order to understand the relationship between current Japanese career women's job-satisfaction and turnover. The participants were divided into 2 groups based on whether or not they had changed jobs. As a result of factor analysis, job satisfaction was summarized into 5 factors : job interest, expectations of women, volume of work, health and welfare benefits, and career development. The scores of the "health and welfare benefits" factor differed significantly between the 2 groups. A hierarchical logistic regression analysis found that low satisfaction with "health and welfare benefits" tended to affect turnover intention. In addition, satisfaction with "job interest" and "volume of the job" tended to influence turnover intention, and at the same time these effects depended on the past turnover experience. From these study results, it is suggested that the current Japanese career women's turnover is mainly affected by the responsibilities of women in the face of the work-family conflict.

Ito et al (2001) examined psychiatric nurses' intention to leave their job in relation to perceived risk of assault, job satisfaction, supervisory support, perception of other job opportunities, and the number of previous job changes. Respondents were 1,494 nurses (mean age 39.2 yrs; response rate, 76.5%) employed in 27 psychiatric hospitals in Japan. 44% reported intention to leave their job, and 89% of those perceived a risk of assault. Younger age, fewer previous job changes, less supervisory support, lower job satisfaction, and more perceived risk of assault were significant predictors of the intention to leave. Organizational efforts are necessary to retain frontline professional staff.

SELF-EFFICACY AND JOB SATISFACTION

In the decade since Staw et al (!986) discovered a link between childhood personality and job satisfaction later in life, there has been a considerable interest in the relationship between individual dispositions and job satisfaction. Although this literature has had its critics, an accumulating body of research suggests that variance in job satisfaction across individuals can be traced to measures of affective temperament (House et al, 1996; Motowidlo, 1996). More recently, researchers have begun to explore the psychological processes that might underlie dispositional sources of job satisfaction. For example, Weiss and Cropanzano (1996) suggested that affective temperament may influence the experience of emotionally significant events at work, which, in turn, influence job satisfaction. Similarly, both Brief (1998) and Motowidlo (1996) have recently offered theoretical models in an attempt to illuminate the relationship between dispositions and job satisfaction.

Continuing this theoretical development, Judge et al (1997) offered a theory linking "core evaluations" of the self to job satisfaction. They defined core self-evaluations as fundamental assessments that individuals make about themselves and their self-worth. Incorporated into their concept of core self-evaluations are four dispositional traits : self-esteem, generalized self-efficacy, locus of control, and low neuroticism. According to Judge et al (1997), these specific traits indicate a single, higher order factor that they argued forms the basis for other, more specific evaluations. In a test of this theory on three diverse samples, Judge et al (1998) demonstrated that individuals with positive self-evaluations were more likely to assess their job satisfaction at higher levels than individuals with less positive self-evaluations. Furthermore, Judge et al (1998) found that the link between core self-evaluations and job satisfied was mediated by perceptions of intrinsic job characteristics. Drawing from Hackman & Oldham (1980), Judge et al, (1998) considered intrinsic job characteristics to include five core job dimensions (identity, variety, feedback, autonomy, and significance). Individuals with positive self-evaluations rated their work as higher on these core dimensions, and thus were more satisfied with their jobs.

Similarly, Judge et al (2000) tested a model of the relationship between core self-evaluations, intrinsic job characteristics, and job satisfaction. The model hypothesized that both subjective (perceived) job characteristics and job complexity mediate the relationship between core self-evaluations and job satisfaction. Two studies were conducted to test the model. Results from Study 1 supported the hypothesized model but also suggested that alternative models fit the data well. Results from Study 2 revealed that core self-evaluations measured in childhood and in early adulthood were linked to job satisfaction measured in middle adulthood. Furthermore, in Study 2 job complexity mediated part of the relationship between both assessments of core self-evaluations and job satisfaction.

CONCLUSION

Research literature amply demonstrates that performance and turnover ought to have a negative relationship (Cotton & Tuttle, 1986; Morrow et al, 1999; Vecchio & Norris, 1996; Dreher, 1982; Martin et al, 1981; Steers & Mowday, 1981) because higher performers are more likely to receive greater rewards and thus be less likely to quit the organization. The meta-analytic evidence supports a moderate negative relationship between performance and turnover (McEvoy & Cascio, 1987; Bycio et al, 1990; Williams & Livingstone, 1994; Hom & Griffeth, 1995). However, Lance (1988) was of the view that performance and turnover might have a positive relationship, because higher performers are likely to have more alternative job opportunities and thus are more likely to be able to leave. Perusal of related research studies reveals that the performance-turnover relationship might be non linear (Jackofsky, 1984; Trevor et al, 1997) or nonexistent (Wright & Bonett, 1993). Some studies have highlighted the mediating role of reward system in the performance-turnover relationship (Johns, 1989; Zenger, 1992; Harrison et al, 1996). They found that high performers are less likely to want to quit when rewards are maximally contingent on performance. Thus, this state of affairs clearly points to the need to investigate the impact of turnover intentions on work performance alongwith other variables which may mediate the relationship between these two variables.

The concept of job satisfaction is central to many aspects of industrial and organizational behaviour. Results of some research studies indicated positive relationship between job satisfaction and job performance (Petty et al, 1984; Khaleque, 1979; Haque, 1991; Hossain, 1995). However, a number of research studies have reported relatively low correlation between job satisfaction and job performance (Brayfield & Crockett, 1995; Iaffaldano & Muchinsky, 1985; Locke, 1976; Vroom, 1964; Keaveney & Nelson, 1993). Review of the literature show equivocal findings, thus, further investigation is required in this area.

Conventional wisdom holds that increasing self-efficacy will result in increases in performance (Bandura, 1982; Stajkovic & Luthans, 1998; Bandura & Wood, 1989; Cervone et al, 1991; Mitchell et al, 1994; Stajkovic & Luthans, 1997). Although a large number of studies reported positive relationship between self-efficacy and performance, but some investigators observed negative relationship when the analysis is done across time (repeated measures) rather than across individuals (Powers, 1973, 1991; Hawkins, 1992; Vancouver et al, 2001; Vancouver et al, 2002). It points to a complex and confusing relationship between self-efficacy and job performance suggesting more probes in the area.

It is clearly evident from the ongoing discussion that most of the earlier research attempts concentrated on investigating the relationship between job performance and turnover intentions, job satisfaction and self-efficacy separately. Further, it may be noted that majority of studies concentrated on bivariate approach which does not account for relative contribution of well known antecedents of work performance. The present study attempts to fill these exiting gaps. The subsequent chapters of the book are devoted to the achievement of the earlier said objectives.

3

CONCEPTUAL FRAMEWORK

INTRODUCTION

Research is a careful inquiry by the way of collection, compilation, presentation and interpretation of the facts, information and data. It is a systematic and purposeful study of a subject and aims to throw a flood of light on the valuable facts. The fundamental purpose of any research is to increase the subject knowledge. The present investigation has been designed to study the work performance of scientists in relation to turnover intentions, job satisfaction and job specific self-efficacy. In order to fulfil research objectives, Shore and Martin's turnover intentions scale, Brayfield and Rothe's index of job-satisfaction, a job-specific self-efficacy scale modelled after Parker, and Randall et al's work outcomes scale were used. The research methodology used to achieve the research objectives has been described in the following sections.

SAMPLE

The present study was conducted on a sample of 300 scientists (150 from National Dairy Research Institute, Karnal and 150 from Agriculture Extension Centres in Haryana). The sample was drawn using simple random sampling procedure. Only the scientists having at least three years of experience in the same organization and educated at least up to post graduate level were included in the sample. They were in the age range of 26 to 65 years.

DESCRIPTION OF THE TESTS

The tests used in this study are :

1. Turnover Intentions Scale by Shore and Martin (1989).
2. Index of Job-Satisfaction by Brayfield and Rothe (1951).
3. A job-specific Self-Efficacy Scale modelled after Parker (1994) by Sood (1999).
4. Work Outcomes Scale by Randall et al (1990).

A brief description of all the four tests is as under :

1. Turnover Intentions Scale

The intent to quit was measured using four items adapted from Hunt et al (1981). The scale assessed the employee's intentions to leave the organization (sample alphas were .78 and .74). The four-item scale adapted by Shore & Martin (1989) has statements that represent possible intentions to quit the organization in near future. The responses for scaled items were rated on a five-point scale (1 to 5).

2. Job Satisfaction Scale

Brayfield and Rothe's Index of job satisfaction (1951) was used to have a precise general measure of job satisfaction of the subjects. It gives an index of "overall" job satisfaction rather than specific aspects of job satisfaction. The scale contained a total of 18 items and the responses of the subjects were measured on a five-point scale.

3. Self-Efficacy Scale

A job-specific Self-Efficacy Scale adapted by Sood (1999) was used to assess the self-efficacy of the subjects. The development of the scale was based on Bandura's (1982) conceptualization of the strength and certainty for performance level. Items for the scale were generated to be consistent with the theoretical formulations of the construct and specific to the beliefs within the respondents' work-setting.

This scale consists of eleven items each relating to general events/circumstances/difficulties, which an individual may encounter in his/her day to day life. Through the responses of these items, the person shows his/her beliefs about his achievements, persistence, problem-solving ability, adaptability and measures to remove obstacles that may come in his/her way while dealing with different circumstances or performing certain activities. The subject is required to give his/her responses by checking one of the five response alternatives arranged into a five-point scale. Each response is scored on a five-point rating scale and a single total score is obtained which is the index of individual's self-efficacy beliefs. The total score of the subject may range between 11 and 55.

4. Work Outcome Scale

The work outcome scale by Randall et al (1990), was used to have a fair assessment of work outcome or work performance of the subjects. The scale consists of six aspects of work outcome in organizational settings, such as work accomplishment, dealing with co-workers, knowledge of work assigned, management of time and resources, sharing knowledge and information with other members and overall work performance. The rater was required to provide rating of work performance on each area on an 11-point rating scale, a score of 1 being the lowest, 11 being the highest, and 6 being the moderate. The subjects made the self rating about themselves. Furthermore, they were clearly told that information provided by them will be used for research purpose and it had nothing to do with the routine evaluation of an employee in the organization.

ADMINISTRATION OF THE TESTS

For the purpose of collecting data for the present study, the subjects were approached personally. The subjects were contacted in their respective departments as well as at their residences and their willingness to participate in the study was sought. They were told at the very outset that it is a part of scientific study and the data collected will be used only for research purpose by the investigator. As most of the subjects were willing to participate in the testing only during their unoccupied (free) time, they were tested individually whenever they were free from their duties. All the four tests were administered according to the prescribed procedure to get appropriate responses.

Although there was no time limit to finish the test, efforts were made to get maximum cooperation of the subjects and they were asked to complete the test as early as possible. The subjects took approximately 50 to 60 minutes to finish all the four tests on the average. The tests were administered in the following sequence : job-satisfaction scale, turnover intention scale, self-efficacy scale and work outcomes scale. On the whole, the subjects were very cooperative.

SCORING

The scoring of the tests was done by following the procedure recommended by the authors of the tests.The turnover intentions scale was scored on a 5-point scale. The specific procedure as suggested by the authors for each of the item was used. The scale contained 4 items, the minimum and maximum possible score is 4 and 20, respectively. The lower the score, the lower is the intention to quit.

The job-satisfaction scale was scored on a 5-point scale. The score for negatively phrased statements was reversed for them. An overall job-satisfaction score was obtained by adding up the individual item score. The higher the score, the greater is the satisfaction. The scale contained 18 items, thus the range of possible total scores is from 18 to 90, with 54 (undecided) the neutral point.

For the self-efficacy scale, items were scored on a five-point scale, indicating the higher the score, the better the self-efficacy. In other words, subjects high score on the self-efficacy scale shows high belief about his efficacy. The score for negatively phrased statements was reversed for it. An overall self-efficacy score was obtained by adding up individual item scores. The scale contained 11 items. Thus, the total score of the subject may range between 11 and 55.

The work outcome scale provided scores on an eleven-point scale. A score of one being the lowest, and eleven being the highest, six being the average. The scale concerned six aspects of work outcome; a single score was obtained by adding up individual item scores to represent an overall work outcome index. As the scale contained 6 items, the minimum and maximum possible score ranges between 6 and 66.

STATISTICAL ANALYSIS

The obtained data were processed for the computation of means, standard deviations, skewness, kurtosis, 't' test, Pearson's correlation and multiple regression analysis.

LIMITATIONS

Limitations are part and parcel of any kind of research work. So, the present study is assumed to be not free from limitations. Although adequate precautionary measures have been taken for the present study, yet the study suffers from some limitations. One of the limitations of the present study was that there are other variables besides turnover intentions, job satisfaction and self - efficacy such as work motivation, organizational commitment, opportunities, communication, etc. which may affect performance of the employees. These could be covered to get a better picture. Secondly, given the correlation nature of the study it is hard to point out the direction of causality. Although the results are consistent with the notions that turnover intentions, job satisfaction and self – efficacy affect work performance this needs to be established through a longitudinal or experimental study. Thirdly, the sample for the present study had been Haryana state based. In order to get more dependable results, the sample could be taken from the other states of the country. For greater validity and generalization further research seems necessary. Nevertheless, the organizations can benefit immensely by adopting appropriate measures, in the context of the present findings, for enhancing performance of their employees and the overall performance of the organization.

4

MEASUREMENT OF WORK PERFORMANCE

Organizations are run through its people. An organization set and achieves its objectives through its employees. Thus the performance of any organization is dependant upon the sum total of the performance of its workers. An organization's success lies in the accurate measurement of the performance of its workforce and uses it objectively to optimize them.

In order to fulfil the main objectives of the present study, the obtained data were analysed statistically in terms of means, standard deviation, skewness, kurtosis, t-test, intercorrelation and multiple regression. The sample for the present study consists of two groups i.e. NDRI scientists (N=150) and scientists at Agriculture Extension Centres in Haryana (N=150). The results obtained after analysis have been presented under five separate headings i.e. Descriptive Statistics, Correlation Analysis, Multiple Correlation and Regression Analysis for the total sample and comparative analysis of both groups of scientists. Lastly, the main findings are given in the end.

DESCRIPTIVE STATISTICS

Frequency distribution for all the nine variables (e.g. five demographic variables i.e. age, qualification, designation, number of dependents and experience; one of job satisfaction, one of turnover intentions, one of self-

Table 4.1: Frequency Distribution of Scores of Age, Qualification, Designation, Number of Dependents and Experience (Scientists : N=300)

C.I	F.D. of *Age*	C.I.	F.D. of *Qualification*	C.I.	F.D. of *Designation*	C.I.	F.D. of *number of Dependents*	C.I.	F.D. of *Experience*
65-69	01	1	48	1	92	0	13	35-39	09
60-64	01	2	252	2	172	1	26	30-34	45
55-59	42			3	36	2	85	25-29	63
50-54	71					3	110	20-24	58
45-49	61					4	42	15-19	51
40-44	55					5	21	10-14	22
35-39	34					6	03	5-9	44
30-34	32							1-4	08
25-29	03								
	300		300		300		300		300
Mean			45.57		1.84	1.81		2.75	20.59
S.D.			8.18		.36	.62		1.33	8.86
Sk			.08		3.44	.02		2.15	.06
Ku			2.21		4.44	2.42		13.67	2.09

C.I. = CLASS INTERVAL

F.D. = FREQUENCY DISTRIBUTION

Table 4.2: Frequency Distribution of Scores on the Measures of Job Satisfaction, Turnover Intentions, Self-Efficacy and Work Performance (Scientists : N=300)

C.I.	F.D. of Job Satisfaction	C.I.	F.D. of Turnover Intentions	C.I.	F.D. of Self-Efficacy	C.I.	F.D. of Work Performance
85-89	06	19-21	01	55-57	02	66-69	13
80-84	15	16-18	10	52-54	06	62-65	31
75-79	48	13-15	20	49-51	39	58-61	102
70-74	83	10-12	55	46-48	69	54-57	77
65-69	88	7-9	90	43-45	83	50-53	43
60-64	38	4-6	124	40-42	69	46-49	24
55-59	06			37-39	24	42-45	08
50-54	11			34-36	08	38-41	02
45-49	03						
40-44	02						
	300		300		300		300
Mean	69.33		7.98		44.37		56.45
S.D.	7.42		3.42		4.16		5.44
Sk	.32		1.70		.06		.25
Ku	4.12		6.26		3.39		3.02

C.I. = CLASS INTERVAL

F.D. = FREQUENCY DISTRIBUTION

efficacy and one of work performance) were set up. These distributions along with their means, standard deviations, skewness and kurtosis are reported in Tables 1 and 2.

A review of Tables 1&2 reveals that the means for demographic variables i.e. age, qualification, designation, number of dependents and experience are 45.57, 1.84, 1.81, 2.75 and 20.59, respectively. Their S.D. are 8.18, .36, .62, 1.33 and 8.86, respectively. The mean scores of the subjects on the measures of job satisfaction, turnover intentions, self-efficacy and work performance are 69.33, 7.98, 44.37 and 56.45, respectively. Their S.D. are 7.42, 3.42, 4.16 and 5.44, respectively. A careful inspection of skewness coefficients reveals that the measure of qualification, number of dependents, job satisfaction, and turnover intentions are positively skewed at .01 level of significance. The measure of work performance is skewed at .05 level of significance. Other distributions are normal. A review of kurtosis coefficients shows that the measure of age, designation and experience are leptokurtic in the distribution of scores whereas the measure of qualification, number of dependents, job satisfaction and turnover intentions are playkurtic in the distribution of scores. Other distributions are normal.

CORRELATIONAL ANALYSIS

Intercorrelations among the scores of all the nine variables (e.g. five demographic variables i.e. age, qualification, designation, number of dependents and experience; one of job satisfaction, one of turnover intentions, one of self-efficacy, and one of work performance) have been computed for the scientists by applying Pearson's product moment method of correlation. The intercorrelation matrix for scientists is reported in Table 3. For 300 scientists correlation coefficient of .113 and .148 are significant at .05

and .01 level of significance. The description of inter-correlations has been presented in different combinations most pertinent to the main objectives of the research.

INTERCORRELATIONS AMONG THE DEMOGRAPHIC VARIABLES

The intercorrelations among the five demographic variables (i.e. age, qualification, designation, number of dependents and experience) are in the range of -.071 to .935. A review of Table 3 reveals that out of the ten intercorrelations only five are significant, others are nonsignificant. The significant correlations are between age and experience (r=.935 P<.01), between age and designation (r=.556 P<.01), between designation and experience (r=.571 P<.01), between designation and qualification (r=.320 P<.01) and between age and qualification (r=.119 P<.05). This shows that age, qualification, and experience share much of their variances with the level of status. This indicates that with the increase in age, qualification and experience the person tends to occupy a high position in the organisation.

INTERCORRELATIONS BETWEEN THE MEASURE OF JOB SATISFACTION AND DEMOGRAPHIC VARIABLES

The intercorrelations between the measure of job satisfaction and demographic variables range from .069 to .227. Out of five, only two intercorrelations are significant i.e. between age and job satisfaction (r=.227 P<.01) and between experience and job satisfaction (r=.175 P<.01). Others are non significant. This shows that with the increase in age and experience a person's job satisfaction also increases.

INTERCORRELATIONS BETWEEN THE MEASURE OF TURNOVER INTENTIONS AND DEMOGRAPHIC VARIABLES

The intercorrelations between the measure of turnover intentions and demographic variables range from -.140 to .057. Out of the five correlations, three are significant. Inspection of Table 3 shows that age is negatively correlated with turnover intentions (r=-.239 P<.01). Experience and designation are also negatively correlated with turnover intentions (r=-.247 P<.01 and r=-.140 P<.05, respectively). This indicates that age, experience and designation play an important role in influencing the intentions of an employee to quit the job whereas qualification and number of dependents do not. The turnover intention scale has been scored in a manner that lower the score, lower is the turnover intention. Thus, the negative correlation reveals that with increase in age, experience and status in the organization the intention to quit decreases significantly.

INTERCORRELATIONS BETWEEN THE MEASURE OF SELF-EFFICACY AND DEMOGRAPHIC VARIABLES

The intercorrelations between the measure of self-efficacy and demographic variables range from -.015 to .067. None of the intercorrelations crosses even the minimum level of .05 significance. This shows that the measure of job specific self-efficacy and demographic variables taken in the present study are functionally independent.

INTERCORRELATIONS BETWEEN THE MEASURE OF WORK PERFORMANCE AND DEMOGRAPHIC VARIABLES

A review of the intercorrelation matrix (Table 3) reveals that intercorrelations between the measure of work performance and demographic variables range from -.036

Table-3: Intercorrelation Matrix (Scientists : N=300)

S.No.	*Variables*	*1*	2	3	4	5	6	7	8	9
1.	Age	–	.119	.556	.058	.935	.227	-.239	.065	.066
2.	Qualification		–	.320	.069	.067	.094	.010	-.044	.008
3.	Designation			–	-.071	.571	.069	-.140	-.018	-.036
4.	Number of Dependents				–	.019	.080	.057	-.015	.042
5.	Experience					–	.175	-.247	.067	.069
6.	Job Satisfaction						–	-.417	.303	.247
7.	Turnover Intentions							–	-.175	-.266
8.	Self-Efficacy								–	.473
9.	Work Performance									–

Note : (i) Correlation .113 is significant at .05 level.

(ii) Correlation .148 is significant at .01 level.

to .069. None of the intercorrelations crosses even the minimum level of .05 significance. This shows that the demographic variables do not share their variances with the measure of job performance.

INTERCORRELATIONS BETWEEN THE MEASURE OF JOB SATISFACTION AND TURNOVER INTENTIONS

The correlation between the measure of job satisfaction and turnover intentions is -.417 which is highly significant at .01 level. This shows that job satisfaction is negatively correlated with turnover intentions i.e. the higher the job satisfaction, the lower is the intention to quit the job.

INTERCORRELATIONS BETWEEN THE MEASURE OF JOB SATISFACTION AND SELF-EFFICACY

It is evident from Table 3 that the correlation between the measure of job satisfaction and self-efficacy is positive and highly significant ($r = .303$ $P<.01$). The positive correlation between job specific self-efficacy and job satisfaction reveals that the belief of the person about performing specific job leads to satisfaction towards that job.

INTERCORRELATION BETWEEN THE MEASURE OF JOB SATISFACTION AND WORK PERFORMANCE

The correlation between the measure of job satisfaction and work performance is positive and highly significant ($r=.247$ $P<.01$). The positive correlation between these two variables shows that satisfied work force tends to be a better performer in organizations.

INTERCORRELATION BETWEEN THE MEASURE OF TURNOVER INTENTIONS AND SELF-EFFICACY

Correlation between the measure of turnover intentions and self-efficacy is -.175, which is significant at .01 level of significance. This shows the negative relationship between the two i.e. higher is the self-efficacy of an employee lower is his intent to quit the job.

INTERCORRELATION BETWEEN THE MEASURE OF TURNOVER INTENTIONS AND WORK PERFORMANCE

The correlation obtained between the measure of turnover intentions and work performance is negative and highly significant (r=-.266) at .01 level of significance. This shows that employees with low intention to quit perform better on the job.

INTERCORRELATION BETWEEN THE MEASURE OF SELF-EFFICACY AND WORK PERFORMANCE

The correlation between the measure of self-efficacy and work performance is positive and highly significant (r=.517 P<.01). This shows that job specific self-efficacy plays an important role in determining the level of performance of employees.

MULTIPLE CORRELATION AND REGRESSION ANALYSIS

The correlations among all the nine variables have been described for the scientists, in the preceding section. Although these correlations best represent the association of work performance with the rest of the variables individually, the multiple correlation is an appropriate statistical technique to assess the degree of relationship between the dependent variable and a combination of

Table 4.4: Parameters/Coefficients in Multiple Regression

(Scientists : N=300)

S.No.	*Predictors*	*Regression Coefficients (b)*	*Mean*
1.	Age	-.034	45.57
2.	Qualification	.752	1.84
3.	Designation	-.768	1.81
4.	Number of Dependents	.197	2.75
5.	Experience	.051	20.59
6.	Job Satisfaction	.025	69.33
7.	Turnover Intentions	-.293	7.98
8.	Self-Efficacy	.563	44.37
	Dependent Measure Work Performance		56.45
	Multiple R=.518 Standard Error of the Measurement	R^2= .26 = 4.65	
	F=13.38	DF = 8 and 291	

independent variables. Thus in order to examine the extent to which the set of all these independent variables predict the variance in work performance, multiple R was worked out. The multiple R was computed taking eight predictor variables i.e. age, qualification, designation, number of dependents, experience, job satisfaction, turnover intentions and self-efficacy, and work performance as a dependent variable (Table 4) for scientists.

MULTIPLE REGRESSION ANALYSIS

In order to have information about the joint contribution of predictors (age, qualification, designation, number of dependents, experience, job satisfaction, turnover intentions and self-efficacy) in determining work performance of scientists, Multiple Regression equation and multiple R have been applied.

The solution for regression equation and for multiple R was carried out by using the SPSS 1996 version. Table 4 presents the values of regression coefficients and means etc. for instant inspection of the results.

A general equation of multiple regression that involves all the predictors (e.g. x_1 to x_8) and one dependent measure (y) can be stated as under :

$$y' = a+b_1x_1+b_2x_2+b_3x_3+\ldots\ldots\ldots\ldots+b_8x_8$$

To complete the regression equation, the value of constant (a) may be computed by using the general formula :

$$a = y'-b_1x_1-b_2x_2-b_3x_3\ldots\ldots\ldots\ldots-b_8x_8$$

By substituting the value of regression coefficients (Table 4) of all the predictors, the regression equation then reads :

Table 4.5: Table of t-ratios

Variables	NDRI Scientists : N=150		Scientists of Agriculture Extension Centres in Haryana : N=150			
	Mean	SD	Mean	SD	t-ratio	Significance Level
Age	46.20	8.40	44.95	7.91	1.33	n.s,
Qualification	1.81	.39	1.87	.34	1.26	n.s.
Designation	1.90	.59	1.72	.64	2.61	.01
Number of Dependents	2.54	1.23	2.97	1.39	2.80	,01
Experience	21.74	9.30	19.43	8.24	2.27	.05
Job Satisfaction	69.01	7.30	69.65	7.52	.73	n.s,
Turnover Intentions	8.07	3.61	7.88	3.21	.48	n.s.
Self-Efficacy	44.50	4.23	44.25	4.09	.52	n.s,
Work Performance	56.09	5.44	56.81	5.42	1.13	n.s,

$y' = a+(-.034x_1)+.752x_2+(-.768x_3)+.197x_4+.051x_5+.025x_6+(-.293x_7)+.563x_8$

By inserting the values given in the table we find :

$a = 56.45-(-.034 x 45.57)-(.752 x 1.84)-(-.768 x 1.81)-(.197 x 2.75)-(.051 x 20.59)-(.025 x 69.33)-(-.293 x 7.98)-(.563 x 44.37)=32.04$

The complete regression equation then reads :

$y' = 32.04+(-.034x_1)+.752x_2+ (-.768x_3) +.197x_4+.051x_5 +.025x_6 + (-.293x_7)+.563x_8$

The regression equation in score form indicates that for every unit increase in age and designation, work performance decreases by .034 and .768 units, respectively, whereas with every unit increase in qualification, number of dependents and experience, work performance increases by .752, .197 and .051 units, respectively. Similarly, the regression coefficients given in Table -4 indicates that for every unit increase in job satisfaction and self-efficacy, work performance increases by .025 and .563 units, respectively, whereas for every unit increase in turnover intentions, work performance decreases by .293 units.

Table-4 reveals that multiple R between the predictor variables and dependent variable is .518. The obtained F-ratio for the significance of multiple R is equal to 13.38. The degree of freedom being 8 and 291, the F is significant beyond .01 level. The finding clearly indicates that the predictor variables such as demographic (e.g. age, qualification, designation, number of dependents, experience), job satisfaction, turnover intentions and self-efficacy jointly predict substantial variance in work performance.

The square of multiple R (R^2) being .26 hereby suggests that all the eight predictors jointly account for only 26% of the total variance in work performance of an employee. This means that 74% of variance in work performance is accounted by the variables other than those included in the present study.

COMPARATIVE ANALYSIS

This section proposes to compare the NDRI scientists with the scientists working at Agriculture Extension Centres in Haryana on the measures of job satisfaction, self-efficacy, turnover intentions, work performance and demographic variables. In order to check the significance of difference between mean scores of these groups on different measures, the 't' test was applied. Further comparison in the pattern of intercorrelation among different measures and comparative analysis of Multiple Correlation and Regression have been carried out.

COMPARISON OF MEAN SCORES OF NDRI SCIENTISTS AND SCIENTISTS AT AGRICULTURE EXTENSION CENTRES IN HARYANA:

To study the significance of difference between mean scores of NDRI scientists and scientists at Agriculture Extension Centres in Haryana on all the nine variables, the 't' test has been applied (Table 5).

NDRI scientists have a higher status as compared to the scientists at Agriculture Extension Centres in Haryana, their mean scores being 1.90 and 1.72 ($t=2.6118$ $P<.01$), respectively. This shows that at NDRI more scientists are working on higher ranks as compared to scientists at Agriculture Extension Centres in Haryana.

Scientists at Agriculture Extension Centres in Haryana have more number of dependents as compared to NDRI scientists (t=2.806 P<.01), their mean scores being 2.96 and 2.54, respectively. The present finding shows that scientists at Agriculture Extension Centres in Haryana have more dependents as compared to NDRI scientists.

NDRI scientists are more experienced as compared to the scientists at Agriculture Extension Centres in Haryana. Their mean scores are 21.74 and 19.43 (t=2.273 P<.05), respectively.

Thus the finding obtained of the present analysis for significance difference between the mean scores of NDRI scientists and scientists at Agriculture Extension Centres in Haryana reveals that NDRI scientists are more experienced and occupy higher positions as compared to scientists at Agriculture Extension Centres in Haryana, though scientists at Agriculture Extension Centres in Haryana have more dependents as compared to the NDRI scientists. However on the other measures i.e. job satisfaction

(t=.73 n.s.), self-efficacy (t=.52 n.s.), turnover intentions (t=.48 n.s.) and work performance (t=1.13 n.s.), both the groups have almost similar scores.

CORRELATIONAL ANALYSIS INTERCORRELATIONS AMONG THE DEMOGRAPHIC VARIABLES :

The intercorrelations among the five demographic variables (i.e. age, qualification, designation, number of dependents and experience), for scientists at NDRI and at Agriculture Extension Centres are in the range of -.012 to .947 and .004 to .923, respectively. A review of Table 6 for NDRI scientists reveals that out of the ten intercorrelations only four are significant at .01 level; none of the other intercorrelations even qualify for the minimum level of significance of .05. These are correlation between age and designation (r=.538 P<.01) and between age and experience

Table 4.6: Intercorrelation Matrix (Scientists at NDRI, Karnal: N=150)

S.No.	*Variables*	*1*	*2*	*3*	*4*	*5*	*6*	*7*	*8*	*9*
1.	Age	–	.044	.538	.063	.947	.114	-.287	.102	.093
2.	Qualification		–	.358	-.123	-.012	.036	.029	-.077	-.080
3.	Designation			–	-.113	.537	.020	-.162	-.024	-.070
4.	Number of Dependents				–	.026	.015	.155	.034	.033
5.	Experience					–	.066	-.312	.092	.075
6.	Job Satisfaction						–	-.333	.296	.271
7.	Turnover Intentions							–	-.147	-.233
8.	Self-Efficacy								–	.517
9.	Work Performance									–

Note : (i) Correlation .160 is significant at .05 level.

(ii) Correlation .210 is significant at .01 level.

Table-7: Intercorrelation Matrix (Scientists at Agriculture Extension Centres in Haryana : N=150)

S.No.	*Variables*	*1*	*2*	*3*	*4*	*5*	*6*	*7*	*8*	*9*
1.	Age	–	.225	.570	.079	.923	.353	-.189	.020	.049
2.	Qualification		–	.317	.244	.192	.154	-.009	.000	.098
3.	Designation			–	.044	.595	.125	-.132	-.022	.013
4.	Number of Dependents				–	.056	.126	-.029	-.051	.032
5.	Experience					–	.311	-.178	.029	.083
6.	Job Satisfaction						–	-.510	.315	.219
7.	Turnover Intentions							–	-.209	-.313
8.	Self-Efficacy								–	.434
9.	Work Performance									–

Note : (i) Correlation .160 is significant at .05 level.

(ii) Correlation .210 is significant at .01 level

(r=.947 P<.01). The other two are the correlation between qualification and designation (r=.358 P<.01) and between designation and experience (r=.537 P<.01).

Inspection of Table 7 for scientists at Agriculture Extension Centres in Haryana reveals that all the intercorrelations are positive. Out of the ten intercorrelations, only three are non-significant. The highest intercorrelation is between age and experience (r=.923 P<.01). This shows that for both groups of scientists most of the demographic variables share much of their variances among themselves. Thus, there is only a slight difference between the pattern of intercorrelations among the measures of demographic variables for these two groups.

INTERCORRELATIONS BETWEEN THE MEASURE OF JOB SATISFACTION AND DEMOGRAPHIC VARIABLES

The intercorrelations between the measure of job satisfaction and demographic variables for scientists at the NDRI and at the Agriculture Extension Centres are in the range of .015 to .114 and .125 to .353, respectively. All the intercorrelations are positive for both groups. As Table 6 reveals, none of the intercorrelations crosses the level of even .05 significance in case of NDRI scientists. This shows that the demographic variables taken in the present study have nothing to do with job satisfaction in case of NDRI scientists whereas a review of Table 7 reveals that in case of scientists at the Agriculture Extension Centres, two highly significant intercorrelations are between age and job satisfaction (.353 P<.01), and experience and job satisfaction (.311 P<.01). This indicates that elder and more experienced scientists at Agriculture Extension Centres tend to be more satisfied with their jobs, whereas these variables do not show any sort of association for NDRI scientists. Thus, the pattern of intercorrelation between the job satisfaction and demographic variables differ for the two compared groups.

INTERCORRELATIONS BETWEEN THE MEASURE OF TURNOVER INTENTIONS AND DEMOGRAPHIC VARIABLES

The intercorrelations between the measure of turnover intentions and demographic variables for scientists at the NDRI and at the Agriculture Extension Centres are in the range of -.162 to .155 and -.009 to -.189, respectively. Table 6 reveals that in case of the NDRI scientists, age is negatively correlated with turnover intentions (r=-.287 P<.01). Experience and designation are also negatively correlated with turnover intentions (r=-.312 P<.01 and r=-.162 P<.05, respectively). Thus age, experience and designation have a significant negative correlation with turnover intentions which indicates that increase in age, experience and designation plays an important role in lowering the intentions of an employee to quit the organisation. Whereas qualification and number of dependents do not have any role in determining the level of turnover intentions.

In case of scientists at the Agriculture Extension Centres in Haryana, Table 7 depicts that all the intercorrelations among turnover intentions and demographic variables are negative. Out of the five intercorrelations, only two are significant at .05 level i.e. correlation between age and turnover intentions (-.189 P<.05), and the second one is between experience and turnover intentions (-.178 P<.05) while others are non-significant. This posits that for scientists at the Agriculture Extension Centres in Haryana, age and experience play an important role in influencing an employee's intention to quit the job/organization i.e. with the increase in age and experience turnover intentions decreases. Thus there is only a slight difference between the pattern of intercorrelations between the measure of turnover intentions and demographic variables for these two groups.

INTERCORRELATIONS BETWEEN THE MEASURE OF SELF-EFFICACY AND DEMOGRAPHIC VARIABLES

The intercorrelations between the measure of self-efficacy and demographic variables for scientists at the NDRI and at the Agriculture Extension Centres are in the range of -.024 to .102 and -.022 to .029, respectively. None of the intercorrelations crosses the level of even .05 significance in both groups. Thus, all the intercorrelations in both groups are non significant. This posits that the measure of self-efficacy and demographic variables taken in the present study are functionally independent for both groups. Thus the pattern of intercorrelations between the measure of self-efficacy and demographic variables is almost the same for the two compared groups.

INTERCORRELATIONS BETWEEN THE MEASURE OF WORK PERFORMANCE AND DEMOGRAPHIC VARIABLES

The correlation between work performance and the measure of demographic variables for the NDRI scientists have been presented in Table 6. The intercorrelations are in the range of -.070 to .093. An inspection of this matrix reveals that none of the correlations has crossed the .05 level of significance. Intercorrelations between work performance and the measures of demographic variables for scientists at the Agriculture Extension Centres are shown in Table 7. The intercorrelation lies in the range of .013 to .098. Again, none of the correlations has crossed the .05 level of significance. Thus the pattern of intercorrelations between the measure of work performance and demographic variables is almost the same for these two groups.

INTERCORRELATION BETWEEN THE MEASURE OF JOB SATISFACTION AND TURNOVER INTENTIONS

An inspection of Table 6 and 7 for the NDRI scientists and scientists at the Agriculture Extension Centres in Haryana, respectively, reveals that the correlations between job satisfaction and turnover intentions for both groups are negative and highly significant at .01 level of significance. For the NDRI scientists r=-.333 (P<.01) and for scientists at the Agriculture Extension Centres in Haryana r=-.510 (P<.01). This shows that for both groups job satisfaction is negatively correlated with turnover intentions. This posits that higher the job satisfaction of an employee the lower is his intention to quit the job in both cases. Thus for both the groups the pattern of intercorrelation between the measure of job satisfaction and turnover intentions is almost the same.

INTERCORRELATION BETWEEN THE MEASURE OF JOB SATISFACTION AND SELF-EFFICACY

A review of Table 6 and Table 7 for scientists at the NDRI and at the Agriculture Extension Centres, respectively, shows that the correlations between job satisfaction and self-efficacy for both the groups are positive and highly significant. For the NDRI scientists r=.296 (P.<.01) and for scientists at the Agriculture Extension Centres in Haryana r=.315 (P<.01). This shows that for both groups job satisfaction has a positive association with self-efficacy. The positive correlation between self-efficacy and job satisfaction for both the groups reveals that the belief of the person about performing a specific job leads to satisfaction with that job. Thus the pattern of intercorrelation between the measure of job satisfaction and self-efficacy is almost similar.

INTERCORRELATION BETWEEN THE MEASURE OF JOB SATISFACTION AND WORK PERFORMANCE

It is evident from Table 6 & 7 that for both groups the intercorrelations between job satisfaction and work performance are positive and highly significant. The correlation between job satisfaction and work performance for the NDRI scientists is .271 (P<.01) and for scientists at the Agriculture Extension Centres is .219 (P<.01). The positive correlation between these two variables in both cases shows that a satisfied workforce tends to be a better performer. Thus there is a similar pattern of intercorrelation between the measure of job satisfaction and work performance in case of these two compared groups.

INTERCORRELATION BETWEEN THE MEASURE OF TURNOVER INTENTIONS AND SELF-EFFICACY

Inspection of correlation matrix for the NDRI scientists (Table 6) shows that the correlation between turnover intentions and self-efficacy is negative and low (r=-.147). It is non-significant as it could not even qualify the minimum level of significance of .05. This shows that for the NDRI scientists the value of correlation -.147 though non significant is indicative of negative direction in the relationship. Whereas the Table 7 reveals that the correlation between turnover intentions and job specific self-efficacy for scientists at the Agriculture Extension Centres in Haryana is -.209, which is significant at .05 level. This posits that for this group, self-efficacy influences the turnover intentions i.e., the higher the job specific self-efficacy, the lower is the intent to quit. Thus the pattern of intercorrelation between the measure of turnover intentions and self-efficacy differs slightly in the two compared groups.

INTERCORRELATION BETWEEN THE MEASURE OF TURNOVER INTENTIONS AND WORK PERFORMANCE

An inspection of Tables 6 & 7 for the NDRI scientists and for scientists at the Agriculture Extension Centres shows that the correlation between turnover intentions and work performance is -.233 (P<.01) and -.313 (P<.01), respectively. Both the correlations are negative and highly significant. This indicates that for both the groups the employees with low intentions to quit perform better on the jobs. A similar pattern of intercorrelation between the measure of turnover intentions and work performance is reported in these two groups.

INTERCORRELATION BETWEEN THE MEASURE OF SELF-EFFICACY AND WORK PERFORMANCE

A review of Tables 6 & 7 for scientists at the NDRI and at the Agriculture Extension Centres shows that the correlation between job specific self-efficacy and work performance is .517 (P<.01) and .434 (P<.01), respectively. Both the correlations are positive and highly significant. This shows that job specific self-efficacy plays an important role in determining the level of performance of any employee in both groups. Thus, a similar pattern of intercorrelation between the measure of self-efficacy and work performance is reported in the two compared groups.

MULTIPLE CORRELATION AND REGRESSION ANALYSIS

The multiple Rs were computed twice taking eight predictor variables i.e. age, qualification, designation, number of dependents, experience, job satisfaction, turnover intentions and self-efficacy and work performance as dependent variable for scientists at the NDRI (Table-8) and scientists at the Agriculture Extension Centres (Table-9).

Table 4.9: Parameters/Coefficients in Multiple Regression (Scientists at Agriculture Extension Centres in Haryana : N=150)

S.No.	*Predictors*	*Regression Coefficients (b)*	*Mean*
1.	Age	-.150	44.95
2.	Qualification	1.937	1.87
3.	Designation	-.654	1.72
4.	Number of Dependents	.095	2.97
5.	Experience	.175	19.43
6.	Job Satisfaction	-.040	69.65
7.	Turnover Intentions	-.441	7.88
8.	Self-Efficacy	.522	44.25
	Dependent Measure Work Performance		56.81
	Multiple R = .513	R^2 = .26	
	Standard Error of the Measurement	= 4.65	
	F=6.31	DF = 8 and 141	

Table 4.8: Parameters/Coefficients in Multiple Regression (Scientists at NDRI, Karnal : N=150)

S.No.	*Predictors*	*Regression Coefficients (b)*	*Mean*
1.	Age	.091	46.20
2.	Qualification	-.174	1.81
3.	Designation	-.919	1.90
4.	Number of Dependents	.080	2.54
5.	Experience	-.056	21,74
6.	Job Satisfaction	.061	69.01
7.	Turnover Intentions	-.204	8.07
8.	Self-Efficacy	.597	44.50
	Dependent Measure Work Performance		56.09
	Multiple R = .553 Standard Error of the Measurement	R^2 = .30 = 4.53	
	F=7.79	DF = 8 and 141	

An inspection of Table 8 & 9 reveals that multiple Rs between the predictor variables and dependent variable for the NDRI scientists and scientists at the Agriculture Extension Centres are .553 and .513, respectively. The obtained F-ratio for the significance of multiple R is equal to 7.79 for the NDRI scientists and 6.31 for scientists at the Agriculture Extension Centres. The degree of freedom being 8 and 141, the F is significant beyond .01 level for both groups of scientists. Thus, the findings clearly indicate that for both groups of scientists, the variables such as demographic (e.g. age, qualification, designation, number of dependents, experience), job satisfaction, turnover intentions and self-efficacy jointly predict a substantial variance in work performance.

However, for scientists at the NDRI and at the Agriculture Extension Centres the square of multiple R(R^2), being .30 and .26, respectively, suggests that all the eight predictors jointly account for only 30% of the total variance in work performance of the NDRI scientists and 26% of the total variance in work performance of scientists at the Agriculture Extension Centres.

MAIN FINDINGS

1. Most of the demographic variables share a large portion of their variances among themselves.
2. The measure of job satisfaction shares its variance with age and experience, and does not share its variance with the rest of the demographic variables.
3. The measure of turnover intentions shares its variance with age, experience and designation and does not share its variance with the rest of the demographic variables.
4. The measure of self-efficacy does not share its variance

with any of the measures of demographic variables.

5. The demographic variables do not reveal any association with work performance.
6. The measures of turnover intentions and job satisfaction share most of their variances among themselves.
7. The measures of job satisfaction and self-efficacy share much of their variances among themselves.
8. The measure of work performance shares much of its variances with the measure of job satisfaction.
9. The measure of turnover intentions shares its variances with the measure of self-efficacy.
10. The measure of turnover intentions shares much of its variances with the measure of work performance.
11. The measure of self-efficacy share most of its variances with the measure of work performance.
12. A set of eight predictors jointly account for the variance in work performance. The contribution of the predictor variables for work performance is 26%.
13. The NDRI scientists are more experienced and enjoy a higher status as compared to the scientists at Agriculture Extension Centres in Haryana.
14. The scientists at Agriculture Extension Centres in Haryana have more number of dependents as compared to the NDRI scientists.
15. The scientists working at NDRI and at Agriculture Extension Centres do no differ significantly in terms of the measures of self-efficacy, job satisfaction, turnover intentions and are almost at par in work performance.
16. While comparing the pattern of intercorrelations between variables undertaken in this study, it was found that there is a slight difference in the pattern of

intercorrelations among the measures of demographic variables for both the groups of scientists.

17. The pattern of correlations between job satisfaction and demographic variables differs for both the groups of scientists.
18. The pattern of intercorrelations between the measure of turnover intentions and demographic variables slightly differs for both the groups of scientists.
19. The pattern of intercorrelations between self-efficacy and demographic variables are almost similar for scientists at Agriculture Extension Centres and at NDRI.
20. The pattern of intercorrelations between work performance and demographic variables are almost similar for both the groups of scientists.
21. The pattern of intercorrelations between job satisfaction and turnover intentions are almost similar for both the groups of scientists.
22. The pattern of intercorrelations between job satisfaction and self-efficacy are almost similar for both the groups of scientists.
23. The pattern of intercorrelations between work performance and job satisfaction are almost similar for both the groups of scientists.
24. There is a slight difference in the pattern of intercorrelations between turnover intentions and self-efficacy for both the groups of scientists.
25. The pattern of intercorrelations between turnover intentions and work performance are almost the same for the two comparable groups.
26. The pattern of intercorrelations between self-efficacy and work performance are almost the same for NDRI

scientists and scientists at Agriculture Extension Centres in Haryana.

27. A set of eight predictors jointly account for the variance in work performance for both the groups. The contribution of the predictor variables for work performance is 30% and 26% for NDRI scientists and for scientists at Agriculture Extension Centres in Haryana, respectively.

5

CONCLUSIONS

The literature on organizational behaviour characterizes work performance as an outcome of the organizational system. Performance is a dependent variable of interest in the study of organizational behaviour because goals and objectives of the organization are measured in terms of performance. As work performance is a complex phenomenon, it depends upon various factors. Among other important factors, turnover intentions, job satisfaction, job specific self - efficacy have been found to be directly relevant to human performance in the organization.

The present study was designed to examine the association of work performance with turnover intentions, job satisfaction and self-efficacy. In general, the results suggest a highly significant relationship between work performance and the other variables. The findings reveal that scientists at NDRI are more experienced and have occupied higher positions in the organization as compared to the scientists at Agriculture Extension Centres in Haryana. On the other hand, scientists at Agriculture Extension Centres in Haryana have more dependents as compared to the NDRI scientists. However, on the other measures i.e. job satisfaction, self-efficacy, turnover intentions and work performance, both the groups have almost similar scores. This may be attributed to the fact that the working conditions, lab facilities and work culture are almost similar for both the groups of scientists.

The findings of the present study reveal that the relationship between turnover intentions and work performance is negative and highly significant. The obtained findings are in conformity with the findings of Dreher, 1982; Martin et al, 1981; Steers & Mowday, 1981; Morrow et al, 1999, who clearly indicate that higher performers are likely to receive greater rewards from the organization and thus be less likely to quit the organization. The above-mentioned findings can also be supported by the meta-analysis results that there exists a moderate negative relationship between performance and turnover (McEvoy & Cascio, 1987; Bycio et al, 1990; Williams & Livingstone, 1994; Hom & Griffeth, 1995).

The relationship between job satisfaction and work performance is fairly unequivocal. The findings of the present study clearly provide evidence of considerable relationship between work performance and job satisfaction. A highly significant positive correlation between these two variables has been obtained. These findings are directly in line with a number of earlier studies on job satisfaction and work performance (e.g. Petty et al, 1984; Khaleque, 1979; Haque, 1991; Hossain, 1995). Therefore, it can be concluded that satisfied workforce tends to be more productive or a higher performer. However, some researchers have reported lower degree of association between job satisfaction and job performance (e.g. Locke, 1976; Herzberg et al, 1957; Vroom, 1964; Lee & Mowday, 1987; Tett & Meyer, 1993).

Some researchers have demonstrated that high level of self-efficacy leads to increased performance of employees (Bandura, 1982; Stajkovic & Luthans, 1997; Bandura & Wood, 1989; Stajkovic & Luthans, 1998; Cervone et al, 1991; Mitchell et al, 1994). The findings of the present study are in line with the findings reported by the above-mentioned researchers. In the present study high positive relation has been obtained between self-efficacy and work performance suggesting thereby that the higher the job specific self-efficacy, the higher will be the work performance. Thus, it can be concluded that in determining the work performance level of employees, job specific self-efficacy plays a significant role.

The intercorrelations between the measure of work performance and the demographic variables (i.e. age, qualification, designation, number of dependents and experience) are non-significant. This suggests that demographic variables such as age, qualification, designation, experience and number of dependents have very little influence on the level of work performance of scientists. The present findings can be supported by McEvoy & Cascio's (1987) meta-analysis result which reveals that age and job performance are generally unrelated. However, Joshi (1993) found that total work experience and number of children are negatively correlated with work performance. Pathak (1982) also found that the demographic variables of age, educational, marital status, length of service, previous work experience and number of dependents were significantly related to job performance and job involvement.

The general character of the findings particularly with regard to predictive value of demographic variables (viz. age, qualification, designation, number of dependents and experience), job satisfaction, turnover intentions and self-efficacy for work performance bears an important implication in the field of organizational behaviour. The results of multiple regression and multiple correlation show that demographic variables, job satisfaction, turnover intentions and self-efficacy jointly account for the variance in work performance. The coefficients of multiple determinants indicate that 26% of the variance in work performance is accounted for by the predicting variables. In sum, measures of demographic variables, job satisfaction, turnover intentions and self-efficacy jointly account for considerable amount of variance in work performance.

Despite the significant correlations between most of the individual predictors with work performance, the multiple non-determinants ($1\text{-}R^2$) are high. This posits that there are certain potent factors, other than those included in the present study, which determine work performance of employees to a greater extent. Thus, it clearly indicates the need of future research in this area by taking certain other variables, personal or organizational in nature.

SUMMARY

The industrial world is becoming increasingly globalized day by day. The organizations are under severe pressure to be innovative and productive so as to remain competitive in the global market. Besides interventions like diversification, technology acquisition and introduction of new systems, it has been observed and also proved by research that eventually much of the result depends upon the human inputs. No wonder, then, that progressive organizations are today more anxious than ever before to get their employees to identify more closely with the organizational objectives and values. Thus it has become necessary for organizations to give special attention to organizational innovation, flexibility, productivity and responsiveness to changing conditions for their survival and success. Moreover, the managers and executives now fully recognize that inculcating a performance-driven culture is the key to success.

There is ample evidence to indicate that performance and turnover ought to have a negative relationship (Dreher, 1982; Vecchio & Norris, 1996; Morrow et al, 1999; Williams & Livingstone, 1994; Hom & Griffeth, 1995). However, other researchers (e.g., Lance, 1988) have argued that performance and turnover might have a positive relationship, because higher performers are likely to have more alternative job opportunities and are thus more likely to be able to leave. Some research studies reveal that the performance-turnover relationship might be non linear (Jackofsky, 1984; Trevor et al, 1997) or nonexistent (Wright & Bonett, 1993). For satisfaction-performance relationship, some research studies indicated positive relationship between job satisfaction and job performance (Petty et al, 1984; Khaleque, 1979; Haque, 1991; Hossain, 1995). However, a number of research studies have reported relatively low correlation between job satisfaction and job performance (Brayfield & Crockett, 1955; Iaffaldano & Muchinsky, 1985; Vroom, 1964; Locke, 1976). Conventional wisdom holds that increasing self-efficacy will result in increases in performance (Bandura, 1982; Stajkovic & Luthans, 1998; Bandura & Wood, 1989; Mitchell et al, 1994). However, some investigators observed negative relationship when the analysis is done across time (repeated measures) rather than across individuals (Powers, 1973, 1991; Vancouver et al, 2001; Vancouver et al, 2002).

Thus, it is clearly evident that though a number of independent studies have been conducted to examine the role of turnover intentions, job satisfaction and self-efficacy in determining the level of work performance and other outcome-related behaviours, very little or no correponding literature exists describing their joint contribution. Given this, the present study is an attempt to examine the relative and combined contribution of turnover intentions, job satisfaction and self-efficacy in the prediction of work performance of scientists.

OBJECTIVES

The main objectives of the study are :

1. To study the relationship between turnover intentions and work performance.
2. To study the relationship between job satisfaction and work performance.

3. To study the relationship between self-efficacy and work performance.
4. To study the effect of turnover intentions on work performance.
5. To study the effect of job satisfaction on work performance.
6. To study the effect of self-efficacy on work performance.
7. To study the joint contribution of turnover intentions, job satisfaction and self-efficacy on work performance.
8. To compare the scientists working at NDRI and at Agriculture Extension Centres in Haryana on the measures of turnover intentions, job satisfaction, self-efficacy, work performance and demographic variables.

METHODOLOGY

In order to fulfil these research objectives, a total of 300 scientists (150 NDRI scientists and 150 scientists at Agriculture Extension Centres in Haryana) were selected. The sample was drawn using simple random sampling procedure. Only the scientists having at least three years of experience in the same organization and educated at least up to post-graduate level were included in the sample. They were in the age range of 26 to 65 years.

For collection of data, all the scientists were contacted individually and all tests used in the present investigation were administered at individual level. The subjects were requested to furnish information about demographic variables. Turnover Intentions Scale, index of job satisfaction, and job-specific self-efficacy scale were administered to get information about the level of turnover intentions, the level of job satisfaction and the job specific self-efficacy. For determining the work outcome, scientists were requested to give self-rating of their work performance on a self-work outcome scale.

The scoring of these tests was done as per the procedure prescribed by the respective authors of these tests, though the analysis most pertinent to the research objectives was correlation analysis and multiple regression. The 't' test to check the significance of differences between means of the groups of scientists on different measures taken in the present study was also applied.

MAIN FINDINGS

1. Most of the demographic variables share a large portion of their variances among themselves.
2. The measure of job satisfaction shares its variance with age and experience, and does not share its variance with the rest of the demographic variables.
3. The measure of turnover intentions shares its variance with age, experience and designation and does not share its variance with the rest of the demographic variables.
4. The measure of self-efficacy does not share its variance with any of the measures of demographic variables.
5. The demographic variables do not reveal any association with work performance.
6. The measures of turnover intentions and job satisfaction share most of their variances among themselves.
7. The measures of job satisfaction and self-efficacy share much of their variances among themselves.
8. The measure of work performance shares much of its variances with the measure of job satisfaction.
9. The measure of turnover intentions shares its variances with the measure of self-efficacy.
10. The measure of turnover intentions shares much of its variances with the measure of work performance.
11. The measure of self-efficacy share most of its variances with the measure of work performance.
12. A set of eight predictors jointly account for the variance in work performance. The contribution of the predictor variables for work performance is 26%.

13. The NDRI scientists are more experienced and enjoy a higher status as compared to the scientists at Agriculture Extension Centres in Haryana.
14. The scientists at Agriculture Extension Centres in Haryana have more number of dependents as compared to the NDRI scientists.
15. The scientists working at NDRI and at Agriculture Extension Centres do no differ significantly in terms of the measures of self-efficacy, job satisfaction, turnover intentions and are almost at par in work performance.
16. While comparing the pattern of intercorrelations between variables undertaken in this study, it was found that there is a slight difference in the pattern of intercorrelations among the measures of demographic variables for both the groups of scientists.
17. The pattern of correlations between job satisfaction and demographic variables differs for both the groups of scientists.
18. The pattern of intercorrelations between the measure of turnover intentions and demographic variables slightly differs for both the groups of scientists.
19. The pattern of intercorrelations between self-efficacy and demographic variables are almost similar for scientists at Agriculture Extension Centres and at NDRI.
20. The pattern of intercorrelations between work performance and demographic variables are almost similar for both the groups of scientists.
21. The pattern of intercorrelations between job satisfaction and turnover intentions are almost similar for both the groups of scientists.
22. The pattern of intercorrelations between job satisfaction and self-efficacy are almost similar for both the groups of scientists.
23. The pattern of intercorrelations between work performance and job satisfaction are almost similar for both the groups of scientists.

24. There is a slight difference in the pattern of intercorrelations between turnover intentions and self-efficacy for both the groups of scientists.
25. The pattern of intercorrelations between turnover intentions and work performance are almost the same for the two comparable groups.
26. The pattern of intercorrelations between self-efficacy and work performance are almost the same for NDRI scientists and scientists at Agriculture Extension Centres in Haryana.
27. A set of eight predictors jointly account for the variance in work performance for both the groups. The contribution of the predictor variables for work performance is 30% and 26% for NDRI scientists and for scientists at Agriculture Extension Centres in Haryana, respectively.

LIMITATIONS AND SUUGESTIONS FOR FUTURE RESEARCH

Limitations are part and parcel of any kind of research work. So, the present study is assumed to be not free from limitations. Although adequate precautionary measures have been taken for the present study, yet the study suffers from some limitations. One of the limitations of the present study was that there are other variables besides turnover intentions, job satisfaction and self - efficacy such as work motivation, organizational commitment, opportunities, communication, etc. which may affect performance of the employees. These could be covered to get a better picture. Secondly, given the correlation nature of the study it is hard to point out the direction of causality. Although the results are consistent with the notion that turnover intentions, job satisfaction and self - efficacy affect work performance this needs to be established through a longitudinal or experimental study. Thirdly, the sample for the present study had been Haryana state based. In order to get more dependable results, the sample could be taken from the other states of the country. For greater validity and generalization further research seems necessary. Nevertheless, the organizations can benefit immensely by adopting appropriate measures, in the context of the present findings, for enhancing performance of their employees and the overall performance of the organization.

BIBLIOGRAPHY

Abelson, M.A., & Baysinger, B.D. (1984). Optimal and dysfunctional turnover : Toward an organizational level model. *Academy of Management Review*, 9, 331-341.

Adams, J.S. (1965). Inequity in social exchange. In L. Berkowitz (Ed.), *Advances in Experimental Psychology*, Vol. 2, 267-299. New York : Academic Press.

Adler, A. (1956). (H.C. Ansbacher & R.R. Ansbacher, Eds.). *The individual psychology of Alfred Adler.* New York : Harper & Row.

Adler, S., & Weiss, H.M. (1988). Recent developments in the study of personality and organizational behavior. *International review of industrial and organizational psychology*, 307-330. Chichester, England : Wiley.

Allen, D.G., and Griffeth, R.W. (2001). Test of a mediated performance-turnover relationship highlighting the moderating roles of visibility and reward contingency. *Journal of Applied Psychology*, 86, 1014-1021.

Aquino, K., Griffeth, R.W., Allen, D.G., and Hom, P.W. (1997). Integrating Justice constructs into the turnover process : A test of a referent cognitions model. *Academy of Management Journal*, 40, 1208-1227.

Arnold, H.J., and Feldman, D.C.(1982). A multivariate analysis of the determinants of job turnover. *Journal of Applied Psychology*. 67, 350-360.

Arthur, J.B. (1994). Effects of human resource systems on manufacturing performance and turnover. *Academy of Management Journal*, 37, 670-687.

Arvey, R.D., Bouchard, T.J., Segal, N.L., & Abraham, L. M. (1989). Job satisfaction : Environmental and genetic components. *Journal of Applied Psychology, 74*, 187-192.

Baird, L.S. (1976). Relationship of performance to satisfaction on stimulating and non-stimulating jobs. *Journal of Applied Psychology*, 61, 721-727.

Bandura, A. (1977). Self-efficacy : Toward a unifying theory of behavioral change. *Psychological Review*, 84, 191-215.

Bandura, A. (1977). *Social learning theory*. Englewood Cliffs, NJ : Prentice-Hall.

Bandura, A. (1982). Self-efficacy mechanism in human agency. *American Psychologist*. 37, 122-147.

Bandura, A. (1986). *Social foundations of thought and action : A social cognitive theory*. Englewood Cliffs. NJ : Prentice-Hall.

Bandura, A. (1988). Organizational applications of social cognitive theory. *Australian Journal of Management*, 13, 137-144.

Bandura, A. (1988). Reflection on nonability determinants of competence. In R.J. sterneberg and J. Kolligian Jr. (Eds.) competence considered : perception of competence and incompetence across the life span. *New haven CT : Yale University Press.*

Bandura, A. (1989). Regulation of cognitive processes through perceived self efficacy. *Developmental Psychology*, 25(5), 729-735.

Bandura, A. (1991). Self-efficacy conception of anxiety. In R. Schwarzer & R.A. Wicklund (Eds.), *Anxiety and self-focused attention* (pp. 89-110). New York : Harwood.

Bandura, A. (1997). *Self-efficacy : The exercise of control*. New York : Freeman.

Bandura, A., & Cervone, D. (1986). Differential engagement of self-reactive influences in cognitive motivation.

Organizational Behavior and Human Decision Processes, 38, 92-113.

Bandura, A., & Jourden, F.J. (1991). Self-regulatory mechanisms governing the impact of social comparison on complex decision making. *Journal of Personality and Social Psychology,* 60, 941-951.

Bandura, A., & Schunk, D.H. (1981). Cultivating competence, self efficacy, and intrinsic interest through self motivation. *Journal of Personality and Social Psychology,* 41, 586-598.

Bandura, A., & Wood, R.E. (1989). Effect of perceived controllability and performance standards on self-regulation of complex decision making. *Journal of Personality and Social Psychology,* 56, 805-814.

Bandura, A., Adams, N.E., Hardy, A.B., & Howells, G.N. (1980). Test of the generality of self-efficacy theory. *Cognitive Therapy and Research,* 4, 39-66.

Bandura, A., Taylor, C.B., Williams, S.C., Medford, I.N., & Barchas, J.D. (1985). Catecholamine secretion as a function of perceived coping self-efficacy. *Journal of Consulting and Clinical Psychology,* 53, 406-414.

Barling, J., & Beattie, R. (1983). Self-efficacy beliefs and sales performance. *Journal of Organizational Behaviour Management.* 5, 41-51.

Becker, T.E., Billings, R.S., Evleth, D.M. and Gilbert, N.L. (1996). Foci and bases of employees commitment : Implications for job performance. *Academy of Management Journal.* 39, 464-482.

Bell, B.S., & Kozlowski, S.W.J. (2002). Goal orientation and ability : Interactive effects on self-efficacy, performance, and knowledge. *Journal of Applied Psychology,* 87, 497-505.

Berkowitz, L., Fraser, C., Treasure, F.P., & Cochran, S. (1987). Pay equity, job gratifications and comparisons in pay satisfaction. *Journal of Applied Psychology,* 27, 544-551.

Berry, L.M. (1997). *Psychology at Work*. San Francisco : McGraw Hill Companies Inc.

Bhagat, R.S. (1982). Conditions under which stronger job performance-job satisfaction relationships may be observed : A closer look at two situational contingencies. *Academy of Management Journal*. 25, 772-789.

Biran, M., & Wilson, G.T. (1981). Treatment of phobic disorders using cognitive and exposure methods : A self-efficacy analysis. *Journal of Counseling and Clinical Psychology*, 49, 886-899.

Blau, G., Merriman, K., Tatum, D.S., & Rudmann, S.V. (2001). Antecedents and consequences of basic versus career enrichment benefit satisfaction. *Journal of Organizational Behavior*, 22(6), 669-688.

Bluedorn, A.C. (1982). A unified model of turnover from organizations. *Human Relations*, 35, 135-153.

Blum, M.L., & Naylor, J.C. (1968). *Industrial Psychology : Its Theoretical and Social Foundations*. New York : Harper and Row.

Borman, W.C., & Motowidlo, S.J. (1993). Expanding the criterion domain to include elements of contextual performance. In N. Schmitt & W.C. Borman (Eds.), *Personnel selection in organizations* (pp. 71-98). San Francisco : Jossey-Bass.

Borofsky, G.L. and Watson, R. (1994). Prediction of early voluntary turnover and job performance : The contribution of a pre-employment screening inventory. *Psychological Reports*. 74, 819-826.

Boudreau, J.W. (1992). Utility analysis for decisions in human resource management. In M.D. Dunnette & L.M. Hough (Eds.), *Handbook of industrial and organizational psychology* (2nd ed., Vol. 2, pp. 621-745). Palo Alto, CA : Consulting Psychologists Press.

Boudreau, J.W., & Berger, C.J. (1985). Decision-theoretic utility analysis applied to employee separations and acquisitions. *Journal of Applied Psychology*. 70, 581-612.

Bouffard-Bouchard, T. (1990). Influence of self-efficacy on performance in a cognitive task. *Journal of Social Psychology,* 130, 353-363.

Brayfield, A.H., & Crockett, W.H. (1955). Employee attitudes and employee performance. *Psychological Bulletin*. 52, 396-424.

Brayfield, A.H., & Rothe, H.F. (1951). An index of job satisfaction. *Journal of Applied Psychology,* 35, 307-311.

Brief, A.P. (1998). Attitudes in and around organizations. Thousand Oaks, CA : Sage.

Brodie, A.S. (1995). Salesforce turnover in direct selling organisations in the United Kingdom and France. Masters Thesis, Keele University.

Brown, I., Jr., & Inouye, D.K. (1978). Learned helplessness through modeling : The role of perceived similarity in competence. *Journal of Personality and Social Psychology,* 36, 900-908.

Brown, S.D., Lent, R.W., & Larkin, K.C. (1989). Self-efficacy as a moderator of scholastic aptitude-academic performance relationships. *Journal of Vocational Behavior,* 35, 64-75.

Brown, S.P., Ganesan, S., & Challagalla, G. (2001). Self-efficacy as a moderator of information-seeking effectiveness. *Journal of Applied Psychology,* 86(5), 1043-1051.

Butler, J.K. (1983). Value importance as a moderator of the value-fulfillment - job satisfaction relationship : Group differences. *Journal of Applied Psychology,* 68, 420-429.

Button, S.B., Mathieu, J.E., & Aikin, K.J. (1996). An examination of the relative impact of assigned goals and self-efficacy on personal goals and performance over time. *Journal of Applied Social Psychology*. 25, 1084-1103.

Bycio, P., Hackett, R.D. and Alvares, K.M. (1990). Job performance and turnover : A Review and meta-analysis. *Applied Psychology : An International Review,* 61, 468-472.

Campbell, J.P., McCloy, R.A., Oppler, S.H., & Sager, C.E. (1993). A theory of performance. In N. Schmitt & W.C. Borman (Eds.), *Personnel selection in organizations* (pp. 35-70). San Francisco: Jossey-Bass.

Campbell, J.P., McHenry, J.J. and Wige, L.L. (1990). Modeling job performance in a population of jobs. *Personnel Psychology,* 43, 313-333.

Campbell, N.K., & Hackett, G. (1986). The effects of mathematics task performance on math self-efficacy and task interest. *Journal of Vocational Behavior,* 28, 149-162.

Caplan, R.D., Vinokur, A.D., Price, R.H., & Van Ryn, M. (1989). Job seeking, reemployment, and mental health : A randomized field experiment in coping with job loss. *Journal of Applied Psychology,* 74, 759-769.

Carlson, R.E. (1969). Degree of job fit as a moderator of the relationship between job performance and job satisfaction. *Personnel Psychology,* 22, 159-170.

Carsten, J.M., & Spector, P.E. (1987). Unemployment, job satisfaction, and employee turnover : A meta-analytic test of the Muchinsky model. *Journal of Applied Psychology.* 72, 374-381.

Cascio, W.F. (1994). Costing human resources (3rd ed.). Boston : Kent.

Cascio, W.F. (1998). *Applied psychology in human resource management.* Upper Saddle River, NJ : Prentice Hall.

Cervone, D., & Wood, R. (1995). Goals, feedback, and the differential influence of self-regulatory processes on cognitively complex performance. *Cognitive Therapy and Research,* 19, 519-545.

Cervone, D., Jiwani, N., & Wood, R. (1991). Goal setting and the differential influence of self-regulatory processes on complex decision-making performance. *Journal of Personality and Social Psychology,* 61, 257-266.

Chen, G., Casper, W.J., & Cortina, J.M. (2001). The roles of self-efficacy and task complexity in the relationships among cognitive ability, conscientiousness, and work-related performance : A meta-analytic examination. *Human Performance,* 14(3), 209-230.

Clegg, C.W. (1983). Psychology of employee lateness, absence, and turnover : A methodological critique and an empirical study. *Journal of Applied Psychology,* 68, 88-101.

Cote, S. (1999). Affect and performance in organizational settings. *Current Directions in Psychological Science,* 8, 65-68.

Cotton, J.A. and Tuttle, J.M. (1986). Employee turnover : A meta analysis and review with implications for research. *Academy of Management Review,* 11, 55-70.

Coverdale, S., & Terborg, J.R. (1980). A re-examination of the Mobley, Horner & Hollingsworth model of turnover : A useful replication (Tech. Rep. No. 80-4). Arlington, VA : Office of Naval Research, Organizational Effectiveness Research Program.

Cropanzano, R., & Folger, R. (1989). Referent cognitions and task decision autonomy : Beyond equity theory. *Journal of Applied Psychology,* 74, 293-299.

Crosby, F. (1984). Relative deprivation in organizational settings. In L.L. Cummings & B.M. Staw (Eds.), *Research in organizational behavior,* Vol. 6, 51-94. Greenwich, CT : JAI Press.

Dachler, H.P., & Hulin, C.L. (1969). A reconsideration of the relationship between satisfaction and judged importance of environmental and job characteristics. *Organizational Behavior and Human Performance,* 4, 252-266.

Dalton, D.R., & Todor, W.D. (1979). Turnover turned over : An expanded and positive perspective. *Academy of Management Review.* 4, 225-235.

Dalton, D.R., & Todor, W.D. (1982). Turnover : A lucrative hard dollar phenomenon. *Academy of Management Review,* 7, 212-218.

Dalton, D.R., Krackhardt, D.M., & Porter, L.W. (1981). Functional turnover: An empirical assessment. *Journal of Applied Psychology.* 66, 716-721.

Dalton, D.R., Todor, W.D., & Krackhardt, D.M. (1982). Turnover overstated: The functional taxonomy. *Academy of Management Review.* 7, 117-123.

DeCharms, R. (1978). *Personal causation : The internal affective determinants of behavior.* New York : Academic Press.

Dittrich, J.E., & Carrell, M.R. (1979). Organizational equity perceptions, employee job satisfaction, departmental absence and turnover rates. *Organizational Behavior and Human Performance,* 24, 29-40.

Dolke, A.M. (2000). Effects of job attitudes on job behaviour and mental health. *Indian Psychological Review,* Vol. 54&55, No. 4, 5-15.

Doll, R.E., & Gunderson, E.K.E. (1969). Occupational group as a moderator of the job satisfaction – job performance relationship. *Journal of Applied Psychology,* 53, 359-361.

Dreher, G.F. (1982). The role of performance in the turnover process. *Academy of Management Journal,* 25, 137-147.

Eden, D. and Zuk, Y. (1995). Seasickness as a self-fulfilling prophecy : Raising self-efficacy to Boost Performance at Sea. *Journal of Applied Psychology.* 80, 628-635.

Ellingson, J.E., Gruys, M.L., & Sackett, P.R. (1998). Factors related to the satisfaction and performance of temporary employees. *Journal of Applied Psychology,* 83, 913-921.

Ellis, R.A., & Taylor, M.S. (1983). Role of self-esteem within the job search process. *Journal of Applied Psychology*, 68, 632-640.

Endler, N.S., Speer, R.L., Johnson, J.M., & Flett, G.L. (2001). General self-efficacy and control in relation to anxiety and cognitive performance. *Current Psychology : Development, Learning, Personality, Social*, 20(1), 36-52.

Ewart, C.K. (1992). Role of physical self-efficacy in recovery from heart attack. In R. Schwarzer (Ed.), *Self-efficacy : Thought control of action* (pp. 287-304). Washington DC : Hemisphere.

Ewen, R.B. (1967). Weighting components of job satisfaction. *Journal of Applied Psychology*, 51, 68-73.

Ewen, R.B. (1973). Pressure for production, task difficulty, and the correlation between job satisfaction and job performance. *Journal of Applied Psychology*, 58, 378-380.

Feltz, D.L., Landers, D.M., & Raeder, U. (1979). Enhancing self-efficacy in high avoidance motor tasks : A comparison of modeling techniques. *Journal of Sport Psychology*. 1, 112-122.

Fishbein, M. (1967). Attitude and the prediction of behaviour. In M. Fishbein (Ed.) *Readings in Attitude Theory and Measurement*. New York : Wiley.

Fishbein, M., & Ajzen, I. (1974). Attitudes toward objects as predictors of single and multiple behavioural criteria. *Psychological Review*, 81, 59-74.

Fisher, C.D. (1980). On the dubious wisdom of expecting job satisfaction to correlate with performance. *Academy of Management Review*. 5, 607-612.

Folger, R. (1987). Reformulating the preconditions of resentment : A referent cognitions model. In J.C. Masters & W.P. Smith (Eds.), *Social comparison, social justice, and relative deprivation : Theoretical, empirical, and policy perspectives*, 183-215. Hillsdale, NJ : Erlbaum.

Folger, R., & Martin, C. (1986). Relative deprivation and referent cognitions: Distributive and procedural justice effects, *Journal of Experimental Social Psychology,* 22, 531-546.

Folger, R., Rosenfield, D., & Rheaume, K. (1983). Role-playing effects of likelihood and referent outcomes on relative deprivation. *Representative Research in Social Psychology,* 13, 2-10.

Folger, R., Rosenfield, D., & Robinson, T. (1983). Relative deprivation and procedural justifications. *Journal of Personality and Social Psychology,* 45, 268-273.

Frayne, C.A., & Latham, G.P. (1987). Application of social learning theory to employee self-management of attendance. *Journal of Applied Psychology,* 72, 387-392.

Gage, M. and Polatajko, H. (1994). Enhancing occupational performance through an understanding of perceived self efficacy. *American Journal of Occupational Therapy,* 48(5), 452-461.

Ganster, D.C. (1989). Worker control and well-being : A review of research in the workplace. In. S. Sauter, J. Hurrell, & C. Cooper (Eds.), *Job control and worker health,* 3-24, Chichester, England : Wiley.

Gardner, D.G., & Pierce, J.I. (1998). Self-esteem and self-efficacy within the organizational context. *Group & Organization Management.* Vol. 23(1), 48-70.

Gecas, V. (1989). The Social Psychology of Self-Efficacy. *Annual Review of Sociology.* Vol. 15, 291-316.

George, J.M. (1992). The role of personality in organizational life : Issues and evidence. *Journal of Management,* 18, 185-213.

Ghiselli, E.E. (1971). Explorations in managerial talent. Pacific Palisades. CA : Goodyear.

Gist, M.E. (1987). Self-efficacy : Implications for organizational behaviour and human resource management. *Academy of Management Review.* 12, 472-485.

Gist, M.E. (1989). The influence of training method on self-efficacy and idea generation among managers. *Personnel Psychology,* 42, 787-805.

Gist, M.E., & Mitchell, T.R. (1992). Self-efficacy : A theoretical analysis of its determinants and malleability. *Academy of Management Review.* Vol. 17, 183-211.

Gist, M.E., Schwoerer, C., & Rosen, B. (1989). Effects of alternative training methods on self-efficacy and performance in computer software training. *Journal of Applied Psychology,* 74, 884-891.

Goldsmith, R.E., McNeilly, K.M., & Ross, F.A. (1989). Similarity of sales representatives' and supervisors' problem-solving styles and the satisfaction-performance relationship. *Psychological Reports,* 64, 827-832.

Goldstein, I.L. (1993). *Training in organizations : Need assessment, development, and evaluation.* Pacific Grove, CA : Brooks/Cole.

Good, L.K., Sisler, G.F., & Gentry, J.W. (1988). Antecedents of turnover intentions among retail management personnel. *Journal of Retailing,* 64(3), 295-314.

Gould, D., & Weiss, M. (1981). Effect of model similarity and Model self-talk on self-efficacy in muscular endurance. *Journal of Personality Psychology,* 3, 17-29.

Graen, G. and Ginsburgh, S. (1977). Job resignation as a function of role orientation and leader acceptance; A longitudinal investigation of organizational assimilation. *Organizational Behaviour and Human Performance,* 19, 1-17.

Grant, K., Cravens, D.W., Low, G.S., & Moncrief, W.C. (2001). The role of satisfaction with territory design on the motivation, attitudes and work outcomes of salespeople. *Journal of the Academy of Marketing Science,* 29(2), 165-178.

Greenberg, J. (1987). A taxonomy of organizational justice theories. *Academy of Management Review,* 12, 9-22.

Greenberger, D.B., Strasser, S., Cummings, L.L., & Dunham, R.B. (1989). The impact of personal control on performance and satisfaction. *Organizational Behavior and Human Decision Processes*, 43, 29-51.

Gustafson, H.W. (1982). Force-loss cost analysis. Appendix of W. Mobley. Employee Turnover : causes, consequences, and control. Reading, Mass : Addison-Wesley.

Hackett, G., & Betz, N.E. (1989). An exploration of the mathematics self-efficacy/mathematics performance correspondence. *Journal for Research in Mathematics Educations*, 20, 261-273.

Hackman, J., & Oldham, G. (1980). *Work redesign*. Reading, MA : Addison Wesley.

Haque, A.B.M.Z. (1991). Quality of working life (QWL) of shift workers in rajshahi and khulna divisions, Unpublished Ph.D. Thesis, Rajshahi University, Bangladesh.

Harrington, D., Bean, N., Pintello, D., & Mathews, D. (2001). Job satisfaction and burnout : Predictors of intentions to leave a job in a military setting. *Administration in Social Work*, 25(3), 1-16.

Harrison, D.A., Viriek, M., & William, S. (1996). Working without a net : Time, performance, and turnover under maximally contingent rewards. *Journal of Applied Psychology*, 81, 331-345.

Harter, J.K., & Creglow, A. (1998). A meta-analysis and utility analysis of the relationship between core GWA perceptions and business outcomes (Working Paper 2.0). Lincoln, NE : Gallup Organization.

Hawkins, R.M.F. (1992). Self-efficacy : A predictor but not a cause of behavior. *Journal of Behavioral Therapy and Experimental Psychiatry*, 23, 251-256.

Hellman, C.M. (1997). Job satisfaction and intent to leave. *Journal of Social Psychology*. Vol. 137(6), 677-689.

Herman, J.B. (1973). Are situational contingencies limiting job attitude-job performance relationships ? *Organizational Behaviour and Human Decision Processes,* 10, 208-224.

Herzberg, F., Mausner, B., Peterson, R.O., & Capwell, D.F. (1957). Job attitudes : Review of research and opinion. Pittsburgh, PA : Psychological Service of Pittsburgh.

Hill, T., Smith, N.D., & Mann, M.F. (1987). Role of efficacy expectations in predicting the decision to use advanced technologies. *Journal of Applied Psychology*. 72, 307-314.

Hochwarter, W.A., Perrewe, P.L., Ferris, G.R., & Brymer, R.A. (1999). Job satisfaction and performance : The moderating effects of value attainment and affective disposition. *Journal of Vocational Behavior,* 54, 296-313.

Hollenbeck, J.R., & Williams, C.R. (1986). Turnover functionality versus turnover frequency : A note on work attitudes and organizational effectiveness. *Journal of Applied Psychology.* 71, 606-611.

Hom, P.W., & Griffeth, R.W. (1991). Structural equations modeling test of a turnover theory : Cross-sectional and longitudinal analyses. *Journal of Applied Psychology,* 76, 350-366.

Hom, P.W., & Griffeth, R.W. (1995). Employee turnover. Cincinnati, OH : South-Western College.

Hom, P.W., & Kinicki, A.J. (2001). Toward a greater understanding of how dissatisfaction drives employee turnover. *Academy of Management Journal,* 44(5), 975-987.

Honda-Howard, M., & Homma, M. (2001). Job satisfaction of Japanese career women and its influence on turnover intention. *Asian Journal of Social Psychology,* 4(1), 23-38.

Hoppock, R. (1935). *Job Satisfaction.* Harper & Row, New York.

Hossain, M.M. (1995). Job satisfaction of commercial bank employees in Bangladesh, Unpublished Ph.D. Thesis, University of Dhaka, Bangladesh.

Hossain, M.M. (1997). Some correlates of performance in manufacturing industries. *Journal of Behavioural Sciences*, 8, 35-41.

Hossain, M.M. and Islam, M.T. (1999). Quality of working life and job satisfaction of government hospital nurses in Bangladesh. *Indian Journal of Industrial Relations*, 34, 292-302.

House, R.J., Shane, S.A., & Herold, D.M. (1996). Rumors of the death of dispositional research are vastly exaggerated. *Academy of Management Review*, 21, 203-224.

Hulin, C. (1991). Adaptation, persistence, and commitment in organizations. In M.D. Dunnette & L.M. Hough (Eds.), *Handbook of industrial and organizational psychology* (2nd ed., Vol. 2, pp. 445-505). Palo Alto, CA : Consulting Psychologists Press.

Hulin, C.L. (1966). Job satisfaction and turnover. *Journal of Applied Psychology*, 50, 280-285.

Hulin, C.L. (1968). Effects of changes in job satisfaction levels on employee turnover. *Journal of Applied Psychology*, 52, 122-126.

Hunt, J.G., Osborn, R.N., & Martin, H.J. (1981). A multiple influence model of leadership (Technical report no. 520). Alexandria, Virginia : U.S. Army Research Institute for Behavioural and Social Sciences.

Iaffaldano, M.T., & Muchinsky, P.M. (1985). Job satisfaction and job performance : A meta analysis. *Psychological Bulletin*. 97, 251-273.

Ito, H., Eisen, S.V., Sederer, L.I., & Yamada, O. (2001). Factors affecting psychiatric nurses' intention to leave their current job. *Psychiatric Services*, 52(2), 232-234.

Ivancevich, J.M. (1978). The performance satisfaction relationship : A causal analysis of stimulating and nonstimulating jobs. *Organizational Behaviour and Human Performance.* 22, 350-365.

Jabri, M.M. (1992). Job satisfaction and job performance among R&D scientists : The moderating influence of perceived appropriateness of task allocation decisions. *Australian Journal of Psychology,* 44, 95-99.

Jackofsky, E.F. (1984). Turnover and job performance : An integrated process model. *Academy of Management Review,* 9, 74-83.

Jackofsky, E.F., & Peters, L.H. (1983). Job turnover versus company turnover : Reassessment of the March and Simon participation hypothesis. *Journal of Applied Psychology,* 68, 490-495.

Jackofsky, E.F., Ferris, K.R., & Breckenridge, B.G. (1986). Evidence for a curvilinear relationship between job performance and turnover. *Journal of Management,* 12, 105-111.

Janssen, O. (2001). Fairness perceptions as a moderator in the curvilinear relationships between job demands, and job performance and job dissatisfaction. *Academy of Management Journal,* 44(5), 1039-1050.

Jewell, L.N., & Segall, M. (1990). *Contemporary Industrial/ Organizational Psychology.* 2nd ed., St. Paul, MN : West Publishing Company.

Johns, G. (1989). Performance and turnover cognitions among managers. *Canadian Journal of Administrative Science,* 6, 37-42.

Joshi, R.J. (1993). Gender differences in determinants of job performance. *Indian Journal of Industrial Relations,* Vol. 28, No. 3.

Judge, T.A. (1993). Does affective disposition moderate the relationship between job satisfaction and voluntary turnover ? *Journal of Applied Psychology,* 78, 395-401.

Judge, T.A., Bono, J.E., & Locke, E.A. (2000). Personality and job satisfaction : The mediating role of job characteristics. *Journal of Applied Psychology,* 85, 237-249.

Judge, T.A., Bono, J.E., Thoresen, C.J., & Patton, G.K. (2001). The job satisfaction-job performance relationship : A qualitative and quantitative review. *Psychological Bulletin*. 127, 376-407.

Judge, T.A., Hanisch, K.A., & Drankoski, R.D. (1995). Human resources management and employee attitudes. In G.R. Ferris, S.D. Rosen, & D.T. Barnum (Eds.), *Handbook of human resources management* (pp. 574-596). Oxford, England : Blackwell.

Judge, T.A., Locke, E.A., & Durham, C.C. (1997). The dispositional causes of job satisfaction : A core evaluations approach. *Research in Organizational Behavior*, 19, 151-188.

Judge, T.A., Locke, E.A., Durham, C.C., & Kluger, A.N. (1998). Dispositional effects on job and life satisfaction : The role of core evaluations. *Journal of Applied Psychology*, 83, 17-34.

Kacmar, K.M. and Ferris, G.R. (1989). Theoretical and Methodological considerations in the age-job satisfaction relationship. *Journal of Applied Psychology*, 74(2), 201-207.

Katzell, R.A., Thompson, D.E., & Guzzo, R.A. (1992). How job satisfaction and job performance are and are not linked. In C.J. Cranny, P.C. Smith, & E.F. Stone (Eds.), *Job satisfaction* (pp. 195-217). New York : Lexington Books.

Kavanagh, D.J., & Bower, G.H. (1985). Mood and self-efficacy : Impact of joy and sadness on perceived capabilities. *Cognitive Therapy and Research*, 9, 507-525.

Keaveney, S.M. and Nelson, J.E. (1993). Coping with organizational role stress : Intrinsic motivational orientation, perceived role benefits, and psychological withdrawal. *Journal of the Academy of Marketing Science*, 21(2), 113-124.

Khaleque, A. (1979). Performance and job satisfaction in short cycled repetitive work, in R.G. Sell and Patrica

Shipley (Eds.) *Satisfaction in Work Design : Ergonomics and Other Approaches,* Taylor and Francis Ltd. London.

Konovsky, M.A., & Cropanzano, R. (1991). Perceived fairness of employee drug testing as a predictor of employee attitudes and job performance. *Journal of Applied Psychology,* 76, 698-707.

Korman, A.K. (1970). Toward an hypothesis of work behavior. *Journal of Applied Psychology,* 54, 31-41.

Kreitner and Kinicki (1998). Organizational behavior. Irvin/ McGraw Hill.

Krishnan, A. and Krishnan, R. (1984). Organizational variables and job satisfaction. *Psychological Research Journal,* 8(1-2), 1-11.

Lance, C.E. (1988). Job performance as a moderator of the satisfaction – turnover intention relation : An empirical contrast of two perspectives. *Journal of Organizational Behavior,* 9, 271-280.

Landy, F.J. (1989). Psychology of work behavior. Pacific Grove, CA : Brooks/Cole.

Larson, J.R., Jr.,& Callahan, C. (1990). Performance monitoring : How it affects work productivity. *Journal of Applied Psychology,* 75, 530-538.

Lawler, E.E. and Porter, L.W. (1967). The effect of performance on job satisfaction. *Industrial Relations,* pp. 20-28.

Lee, T.W. (1996). Family characteristics and the prediction of voluntary employee turnover. *Paper presented at the annual meeting of the Academy of Management, Cincinnati.*

Lee, T.W. and Mitchell, T.R. (1994). An alternative approach : The unfolding model of voluntary turnover. *Academy of Management Review,* 19, 51-89.

Lee, T.W. and Mowday, R.T. (1987). Voluntarily living an organization : An empirical investigation of stress and mowdays model of turnover. *Academy of Management Journal,* 721-743.

Lent, R.W., Brown, S.D., & Hackett, G. (1994). Toward a unifying social cognitive theory of career and academic interest, choice, and performance. *Journal of Vocational Behavior Monograph,* 45, 79-122.

Lent, R.W., Brown, S.D., & Larkin, K.C. (1987). Comparison of three theoretically derived variables in predicting career and academic behaviour : Self-efficacy, interest congruence, and consequence thinking. *Journal of Counseling Psychology*. 34, 293-298.

Lind, E.A., & Tyler, T.R. (1988). *The social psychology of procedural justice.* New York : Plenum Press.

Lindsley, Dana H., Brass Daniel, J. and Thomas, James B. (1995). Efficacy-performance spirals : A multilevel perspective. *Academy of Management Review,* 20(3).

Lindstorm, K. (1988). Age-related differences in job characteristics and in their relation to job satisfaction. *Scandinavian Journal of Work, Environment and Health,* 14(1), 24-26.

Litt, M.D. (1988). Self-efficacy and perceived control : Cognitive mediators of pain tolerance. *Journal of Personality and Social Psychology,* 54, 149-160.

Locke, E.A. (1968). Towards a theory of task motivation and incentives. *Organizational Behaviour and Human Performance.* 3, 157-189.

Locke, E.A. (1969). What is job satisfaction ? *Organizational Behaviour and Human Performance,* 4, 309-336.

Locke, E.A. (1970). Job satisfaction and job performance : A theoretical analysis. *Organizational Behavior and Human Performance,* 5, 484-500.

Locke, E.A. (1973). Satisfiers and dissatisfiers among white and blue collar employees. *Journal of Applied Psychology,* 58, 67-76.

Locke, E.A. (1976). The nature and causes of job satisfaction. In M.D. Dunnette (Ed.), Handbook of industrial and organizational psychology. 1297-1349. Chicago : Rand McNally.

Locke, E.A., & Latham, G.P. (1990). *A theory of goal setting and task performance.* Englewood Cliffs, NJ : Prentice-Hall.

Locke, E.A., Fitzpatrick, W., & White, F.M. (1983). Job satisfaction and role clarity among university and college faculty. *Review of Higher Education,* 6, pp. 343-365.

Locke, E.A., Frederick, E., Lee, C., & Bobko, P. (1984). Effect of self-efficacy, goals, and task strategies on task performance. *Journal of Applied Psychology.* 69, 241-251.

Lord, R.G. and Hohenfeld, J.A. (1978). Longitudinal field assessment of equity effects on the performance of major league baseball players. *Journal of Applied Psychology,* 11, 317-332.

Lui, S.S., Ngo, H.Y., & Tsang, A.W.N. (2001). Interrole conflict as a predictor of job satisfaction and propensity to leave : A study of professional accountants. *Journal of Managerial Psychology,* 16(6), 469-484.

Lum, L., Kervin, J., Clark, K., & Reid, F. (1998). Explaining nursing turnover intent : Job satisfaction, pay satisfaction, or organizational commitment ? *Journal of Organizational Behavior,* 19(3), 305-320.

Luzzo, D.A. and Ward, B.E. (1995). The relative contributions of self efficacy and locus of control to the prediction of vocational congruence. *Journal of Career Development,* 21(4).

Mangos, P.M., & Steele-Johnson, D. (2001). The role of subjective task complexity in goal orientation, self-efficacy, and performance relations. *Human Performance,* 14(2), 169-186.

March, J.G., & Simon, H.A. (1958). *Organizations.* New York : Wiley.

Martin, J. (1981). Relative deprivation : A theory of distributive justice for an era of shrinking resources. In L.L. Cummings & B.M. Staw (Eds.), *Research in organizational behavior*, vol. 3 : 53-108, Greenwich, CT : JAI Press.

Martin, T.N., Price, J.L., & Mueller, C.W. (1981). Job performance and turnover. Journal of Applied Psychology, 66, 116-119.

Martinko, M.J. and Gardner, W.L. (1982). Learned Helplessners : An alternative explanation for performance deficits. *Academy of Management Review*, 195-204.

Mathieu, J.E. and Button, S.B. (1992). An examination of the relative impact of normative information and self efficacy on personal goals and performance over time. *Journal of Applied Social Psychology*, 22(22), 1758-1775.

McBey, K. (1996). Exploring the role of individual job performance within a multivariate investigation into part-time turnover processes. *Psychological Reports* : 78, 223-233.

McDonald, T. and Siegall, N. (1992). The effects of technological self efficacy and job-focus on job performance, attitudes and withdrawal behaviour. *Journal of Psychology*, 126(5), 465-475.

McElroy, J.C., Morrow, P.C., & Rude, S.N. (2001). Turnover and organizational performance : A comparative analysis of the effects of voluntary, involuntary, and reduction-in-force turnover. *Journal of Applied Psychology*, 86, 1294-1299.

McEvoy, G.M., & Cascio, W.F. (1985). Strategies for reducing employee turnover : A meta-analysis. *Journal of Applied Psychology*, 70, 342-353.

McEvoy, G.M., & Cascio, W.F. (1987). Do good or poor performers leave ? A meta-analysis of the relationship between performance and turnover. *Academy of Management Journal*, 30, 744-762.

Michaels, C.E., & Spector, P.E. (1982). Causes of employee turnover : A test of the Mobley, Griffeth, Hand, and

Meglino model. *Journal of Applied Psychology*, 67, 53-59.

Mikes, P.S. and Hulin, C.L. (1968). Use of importance as a weighting component of job satisfaction. *Journal of Applied Psychology*, 56, 95-105.

Miller, H.E. (1981). Withdrawal behaviors among hospital employees. Unpublished doctoral dissertation, University of Illinois at Urbana-Champaign.

Miller, H.E. (1982, August). Some evidence concerning the progression of withdrawal hypothesis. Paper presented at the Annual Meeting of the Academy of Management, New York.

Miller, H.E., Katerberg, R., Hulin, C.L. (1979). Evaluation of the Mobley, Horner, and Hollingsworth model of employee turnover. *Journal of Applied Psychology*, 64, 509-517.

Miller, M. (1993). Efficacy strength and performance in competitive swimmers of different skill level. *International Journal of Sport Psychology*, 24(3).

Mitchell, T.R. and Larson, J.R. Jr. (1987). *People in Organizations*, 3rd ed., McGraw-Hill, New York, p. 146.

Mitchell, T.R., Hopper, H., Daniels, D., George-Falvy, J., & James, L.R. (1994). Predicting self-efficacy and performance during skill acquisition. *Journal of Applied Psychology*, 79, 506-517.

Mobley, W.H. (1977). Intermediate linkages in the relationship between job satisfaction and employee turnover. *Journal of Applied Psychology*, 62, 237-240.

Mobley, W.H. (1982). Employee turnover : causes, consequences, and control. Reading, Mass : Addison-Wesley.

Mobley, W.H., Griffeth, R.W., Hand, H.H., & Meglino, B.M. (1979). Review and conceptual analysis of the employee turnover process. *Psychological Bulletin*, 86, 493-522.

Mobley, W.H., Horner, S.O., & Hollingsworth, A.T. (1978). An evaluation of precursors of hospital employee turnover. *Journal of Applied Psychology,* 63, 408-414.

Mone, M.A. (1994). Relationships between self-concepts, aspirations, emotional responses, and intent to leave a downsizing organization. *Human Resource Management,* 33, 281-298.

Mone, M.A., Baker, D.D. and Jeffries, F. (1996). Predictive validity and time dependency of self efficacy, self esteem, personal goals and academic performance. *Educational and Psychological Measurement,* 55(5), 716-727.

Morrow, P.C., McElroy, J.C., Laezniak, K.S., & Fenton, J.B. (1999). Using absenteeism and performance to predict employee turnover : Early detection through company records. *Journal of Vocational Behavior,* 55, 358-374.

Mossholder, K.W., Bedeian, A.G., Niebuhr, R.E., & Wesolowski, M.A. (1994). Dyadic duration and the performance-satisfaction relationship : A contextual perspective. *Journal of Applied Social Psychology,* 24, 1251-1269.

Motowidlo, S.J. (1996). Orientation toward the job and organization. In K.R. Murphy (Ed.), *Individual differences and behavior in organizations* (pp. 175-208). San Francisco : Jossey Bass.

Mowday, R.T., Koberg, C.S., & McArthur, A.W. (1984). The psychology of the withdrawal process : A cross-validational test of Mobley's intermediate linkage model of turnover in two samples. *Academy of Management Journal,* 27, 79-94.

Mowday, R.T., Porter, L.W., & Steers, R.M. (1982). Employee-organization linkages : The psychology of commitment, absenteeism, and turnover. New York : *Academic Press.*

Nagy, M.S. (2002). Using a single-item approach to measure facet job satisfaction. *Journal of Occupational and Organizational Psychology,* 75, 77-86.

Nayyar, M.R. (1994). Some correlates of work performance perceived by first line supervisor : A study. *Management and Labour Studies*, 19, 1, 50-54.

Norris, D.R., & Niebuhr, R.E. (1984). Organization tenure as a moderator of the job satisfaction – job performance relationship. *Journal of Vocational Behavior*, 24, 169-178.

O'Reilly, C.A. (1991). Organizational behavior : Where we've been, where we're going. In M. Rosenzweig & L. Porter (Eds.). *Annual Review of Psychology*, 427-458. Palo Alto, CA : Annual Reviews.

Oldham, G.R. and Cummings, A. (1996). Employee Creativity : Personal and contextual factors at work. *Academy of Management Journal*, 39, 607-634.

Olsen, D. (1993). Work satisfaction and stress in the first and third year of academic appointment. *Journal of Higher Education*, 64, pp. 453-471.

Organ, D.W. (1988). A restatement of the satisfaction-performance hypothesis. *Journal of Management*, 14, 547-557.

Orpen, C. (1995). Self efficacy beliefs and job performance among Black managers in South Africa. *Psychological Reports*, 76(2), 649-650.

Ostroff, C. (1992). The relationship between satisfaction, attitudes, and performance : An organizational level analysis. *Journal of Applied Psychology*, 77, 963-974.

Ostroff, C. (1993). Comparing correlations based on individual-level and aggregated data. *Journal of Applied Psychology*, 78, 569-582.

Ostroff, C., & Schmitt, N. (1993). Configurations of organizational effectiveness and efficiency. *Academy of Management Journal*, 36, 1345-1361.

Packard and Thomas (1989). Participation in decision making, performance, and job satisfaction in a social work bureaucracy. *Administration in Social Work*, 13, pp. 59-75.

Park, H.Y., Ofori-Dankworth, J., & Bishop, D.R. (1994). Organizational and environmental determinants of functional and dysfunctional turnover : Practical and research implications. *Human Relations, 47*, 353-366.

Parker, L.E. (1994). Working together : Perceived self and collective efficacy at the work place. *Journal of Applied Social Psychology*, 24(1).

Pathak, R.D. (1982). Job involvement : Its relationships to certain variables among bank officers in India. *Prajnan*, 11(4), 269-282.

Pettijohn, C.E., Pettijohn, L.S., & d' Amico, M. (2001). Characteristics of performance appraisals and their impact on sales force satisfaction. *Human Resource Development Quarterly*, 12(2), 127-146.

Petty, M.M., McGee, G.W., & Cavender, J.W. (1984). A meta-analysis of the relationships between individual job satisfaction and individual performance. *Academy of Management Review*, 9, 712-721.

Phillips, I.D., (1990). The price tag of turnover. *Personnel Journal*, 58-60.

Podsakoff, P.M., & Farh, J. (1989). Effects of feedback sign and creditability on goal setting and task performance. *Organizational Behavior and Human Decision Processes*, 44, 45-67.

Podsakoff, P.M., & Williams, L.J. (1986). The relationship between job performance and job satisfaction. In E.A. Locke (Ed.), *Generalizing from laboratory to field settings*, 207-253. Lexington, MA : Lexington Press.

Porter, L.W. and Steers, R.M. (1973). Organizational, Work, personal factors in employee turnover and absenteeism. *Psychological Bulletin*, 80, 161-176.

Porter, L.W., & Lawler, E.E. (1968). Managerial attitudes and performance. Homewood. IL : Irwin.

Powers, W.T. (1973). Behavior : The control of perception. Chicago : Aldine.

Powers, W.T. (1991). Commentary on Bandura's "Human Agency". *American Psychologist,* 46, 151-153.

Price, J.L., & Mueller, C.W. (1986). *Absenteeism and turnover of hospital employees.* Greenwich, CT : JAI press.

Randall, D.M., Fedor, D.B., & Longenecker, C.O. (1990). The behaviour expression of organizational commitment. *Journal of Vocational Behaviour,* 36, 210-224.

Renn, R.W., & Fedor, D.B. (2001). Development and field test of a feedback seeking, self-efficacy, and goal setting model of work performance. *Journal of Management,* 27(5), 563-583.

Rhodes, S.R. and Doering, M. (1983). An Integrated model of career change. *Academy of Management Review,* 8, 631-639.

Roberts, H. (1966). Dictionary of Industrial Relations, PNA : Washington.

Robertson, I.T., & Sadri, G. (1993). Managerial self-efficacy and managerial performance. *British Journal of Management,* 4, 37-45.

Roethlisberger, F.J., & Dickson, W.J. (1939). Management and the worker. Cambridge, MA : Harvard University Press.

Romanoff, K.E. (1989). The ten commandments of performance management. *Personnel,* 66(1), 24-28.

Rotter, J.B. (1966). Generalized expectancies for internal versus external control of reinforcement. *Psychological Monographs,* 80, (1, Whole No. 609).

Rubin, R.B., Martin, M.M., Burning, S.S., & Powers, D.E. (1993). Test of a self efficacy model of interpersonal communication competence. *Communication quarterly,* pp. 210-220.

Rusbult, C.E. and Farrell, D. (1983). A longitudinal test of the investment model : The impact on job satisfaction, job commitment, and turnover of variations in rewards, costs, alternatives and investments. *Journal of Applied Psychology,* 68, 429-438.

Russ, F.A. and McNeilly, K.M. (1995). Links among satisfaction, commitment and turnover intentions : The moderating effect of experience, gender and performance. *Journal of Business Research,* 34, 57-65.

S.P.S.S. (1996). *Statistical Package for Social Sciences.* Standard Version, 7.5.1 for Windows Inc.

Sadri, G. and Robertson, I.T. (1993). Self efficacy and work related behaviour : A review and meta analysis. *Applied Psychology,* 42(2), 139-152.

Saks, A.M. (1995). Longitudinal field investigation of the moderating and mediating effects of self-efficacy on the relationship between training and newcomer adjustment. *Journal of Applied Psychology,* 80, 211-225.

Saks, A.M. (1995). Moderating effects of self efficacy for the relationship between training method and anxiety and stress reactions of newcomers. *Journal of Organizational Behaviour.*

Saks, A.M., Mudrack, P.E., & Ashforth, B. (1996). The relationship between the work ethic, job attitudes, intentions to quit, and turnover for temporary service employees. *Canadian Journal of Administrative. Sciences.* v13n3: 226-236.

Sanna, L.J., & Pusecker, P.A. (1994). Self efficacy valence of self evaluation and performance. *Personality and Social Psychology Bulletin,* 20(1).

Scarpello, V., & Campbell, J.P. (1983). Job satisfaction : Are all the parts there ? *Personnel Psychology,* 36, 577-600.

Schaubroeck, J., & Merritt, D. (1997). Divergent effects of job control on coping with work stressors : The key role of self-efficacy. *Academy of Management Journal,* 40, 738-754.

Schaubroeck, J., Xie, J.L., & Lam, S.S.K. (2000). Collective efficacy versus self-efficacy in coping responses to stressors and control : A cross-cultural study. *Journal of Applied Psychology,* 85, 512-525.

Schnake (1991). Organizational citizenship : A review, proposed model and research agenda. *Human Relations,* 44, 735-759.

Schunk, D.H. (1987). Peer models and children's behavioral change. *Review of Educational Research,* 57, 149-174.

Schunk, D.H. (1989). Self-efficacy and achievement behaviors. *Educational Psychology Review,* 1, 173-208.

Schunk, D.H. (1995). Self-efficacy and education and instruction. In J. Maddux (Ed.), *Self-efficacy, adaptation, and adjustment : Theory, research, and application,* 281-303. New York : Plenum Press.

Schunk, D.H. and Gunn, T.P. (1986). Self-efficacy and skill development. Influence of task strategies and attributions. *Journal of Educational Research,* 79, 238-244.

Schwab, D.P. (1991). Contextual variables in employee performance-turnover relationships. Academy of Management Journal, 34, 966-975.

Schwab, D.P., & Cummings, L.L. (1970). Theories of performance and satisfaction : A review. *Industrial Relations,* 9, 408-430.

Schwepker, C.H. Jr. (2001). Ethical climate's relationship to job satisfaction, organizational commitment, and turnover intention in the salesforce. *Journal of Business Research,* 54(1), 39-52.

Sharma, B.R. and Bhaskar, S. (1991a). Determinants of job satisfaction among engineers in public sector undertaking. *ASCI Journal of Management,* 20(4), 217-233.

Shea, C.M., & Howell, J.M. (2000). Efficacy-performance spirals : An empirical test. *Journal of Management,* 26(4), 791-812.

Shell, D.F., Murphy, C.C., & Bruning, R.H. (1989). Self-efficacy and outcome expectancy mechanism in reading and writing achievement. *Journal of Educational Psychology,* 81, 91-100.

Sheridan, J.E. (1985). A Catastrophe model of employee withdrawal leading to low job performance, high absenteeism, and job turnover during the first year of employment. *Academy of Management Journal,*28, 88-109.

Shore, L.M., & Martin, H.J. (1989). Job satisfaction and organizational commitment in relation to work performance and turnover intentions. *Human Relations,* 42, 625-638.

Smith, E.M., Ford, J.K., & Kozlowski, S.W.J. (1997). Building adaptive expertise : Implications for training design. In M.A. Quinones & A. Duda (Eds.), *Training for a rapidly changing workplace : Applications of psychological research* (pp. 89-118). Washington DC : American Psychological Association.

Smith, P.C. (1963). Cornell studies of job satisfaction : Strategy for development of job satisfaction. Unpublished manuscript. Cornell University, cited in Pathak (1983). Organization behaviour in a changing environment.

Smith, P.C., Kendall, L.M., & Hulin, C.L. (1969). *The measurement of satisfaction in work and retirement.* Chicago : Rand McNally.

Snyder, R.A. and Mayo, F. (1991). Single versus multiple causes of the age/job satisfaction relationship. *Psychological Reports,* 68(3), 1255-1262.

Sood, S. (1999). Organizational commitment, work motivation, and perceived self-efficacy as predictors of work outcomes at different job hierarchies in an industrial set-up. *Unpublished Doctoral Thesis,* Department of Psychology, Kurukshetra University, Kurukshetra.

Spector, P.E. (1997). Job satisfaction : Application, assessment, causes, and consequences. Thousand Oaks, CA : Sage.

Spencer, D.G., & Steers, R.M. (1981). Performance as a moderator of the job-satisfaction – turnover relationship. *Journal of Applied Psychology,* 66, 511-514.

Stajkovic, A. and Luthans, F. (1997). Self-efficacy and task performance : A meta-analysis. *Organizational Behavior Division, Academy of Management, Boston.*

Stajkovic, A.D., & Luthans, F. (1998). Self-efficacy and work-related performance : A meta-analysis. *Psychological Bulletin,* Vol. 124(2), 240-261.

Staw, B.M. (1980). The consequences of turnover. *Journal of Occupational Behaviour,* 1, 253-273.

Staw, B.M. (1984). Organization Behaviour : A review and reformulation of the field's outcome variables. *Annual Review of Psychology,* 35, 627-666.

Staw, B.M., Bell, N.E., & Clausen, J.A. (1986). The dispositional approach to job attitudes : A lifetime longitudinal test. *Administrative Science Quarterly,* 31, 56-77.

Steele, R.P., & Ovalle, N.K. (1984). A review and meta-analysis of research on the relationship between behavioral intentions and employee turnover. *Journal of Applied Psychology,* 69, 673-686.

Steele-Johnson, D., Beauregard, R.S., Hoover, P.B., Schmidt, A.M. (2000). Goal orientation and task demand effects on motivation, affect, and performance. *Journal of Applied Psychology,* 85, 724-738.

Steers, R.M. (1975). Effects of need for achievement on the job performance – job attitude relationship. *Journal of Applied Psychology,* 60, 678-682.

Steers, R.M., & Mowday, R.T. (1981). Employee turnover and postdecision accommodation processes. In L.L. Cummings & B.M. Staw (Eds.). *Research in*

Organizational Behavior, (Vol. 3, pp. 235-281). Greenwich, CT : JAI Press.

Stevens, C.K., Bavetta, A.G., and Gist, M.E. (1993). Gender differences in the acquisition of salary negotiation skills : The role of goals, self-efficacy, and perceived control. *Journal of Applied Psychology,* 723-735.

Stone, D.N. (1994). Overconfidence in initial self-efficacy judgements : Effects on decision processes and performance. *Organizational Behavior and Human Decision Processes,* 59, 452-474.

Stumpf, S.A. and Hartman, K. (1984). Individual exploration to organizational commitment or withdrawal. *Academy of Management Journal,* 27, 308-329.

Stumpf, S.A., & Rabinowitz, S. (1981). Career stage as a moderator of performance with facets of job satisfaction and role perceptions. *Journal of Vocational Behavior,* 18, 202-218.

Stumpf, S.A., Brief, A.P., & Hartman, K. (1987). Self-efficacy expectations and coping with career-related events. *Journal of Vocational Behaviour,* 31, 91-108.

Sturman, M.C. and Trevor, C.O. (2001). The implications of linking the dynamic performance and turnover literatures. *Journal of Applied Psychology,* 86, 684-696.

Sundstrom, F. (1986). *Work Places.* New York. Cambridge Univ. Press.

Taylor, M.S., Locke, E.A., Lee, C., & Gist, M.E. (1984). Type A behaviour and faculty research productivity : What are the mechanisms ? *Organizational Behaviour and Human Decision Processes,* 34, 402-418.

Tett, R.P. and Meyer, J.P. (1993). Job satisfaction, organizational commitment, turnover intention and turnover : Path analysis based on meta analytic findings. *Personnel Psychology,* 45, 259-293.

Thibaut, J.W., & Walker, L. (1975). *Procedural justice : A psychological analysis.* Hillsdale, NJ : Erlbaum.

Trempe, J., Rigny, A.J., & Haccoun, R.P. (1985). Subordinate satisfaction with male and female managers. Role of perceived supervisory influence. *Journal of Applied Psychology*, 70, 44-47.

Trevor, C.O. (2001). Interactions among actual ease-of-movement determinants and job satisfaction in the prediction of voluntary turnover. *Academy of Management Journal*, 44(4), 621-638.

Trevor, C.O., Gerhart, B. and Boudreau, J.W. (1997). Voluntary turnover and job performance : Curvilinearity and the moderating influences of salary growth and promotions. *Journal of Applied Psychology*, 82, 44-61.

Vance, R.J., & Colella, A. (1990). Effects of two types of feedback on goal acceptance and personal goals. *Journal of Applied Psychology*, 68-76.

Vancouver, J.B., Thompson, C.M., & Williams, A.A. (2001). The changing signs in the relationships among self-efficacy, personal goals, and performance. *Journal of Applied Psychology*, 86, 605-620.

Vancouver, J.B., Thompson, C.M., Tischner, E.C., & Putka, D.J. (2002). Two studies examining the negative effect of self-efficacy on performance. *Journal of Applied Psychology*, 87, 506-516.

Varca, P.E., & James-Valutis, M. (1993). The relationship of ability and satisfaction to job performance. *Applied Psychology : An International Review*, 42, 265-275.

Vasil, V. (1993). Self efficacy expectations and causal attributions for achievement among male and female university faculty. *Journal of Vocational Behaviour*, 41(3), 259-269.

Vecchio, R., & Norris, W. (1996). Predicting employee turnover from performance, satisfaction, and leader-member exchange. *Journal of Business and Psychology*, 11, 113-125.

Vroom, V.H. (1964). Work and motivation. New York : Wiley.

Waldersee, R. (1994). Self-efficacy and performance as a function of feedback sign and anxiety : A service experiment. *Journal of Applied Psychology,* 30, 346-356.

Waldersee, R., & Luthans, F. (1994). The impact of positive and corrective feedback on customer service performance. *Journal of Organizational Behavior,* 15, 83-95.

Walster, E., Walster, G.W., & Berscheid, E. (1978). *Equity : Theory and research.* Boston : Allyn & Bacon.

Wanous, J.P. and Lawler, E.E. (1972). Measurement and meaning of job satisfaction. *Journal of Applied Psychology,* 56, 95-105.

Wanous, J.P., Sullivan, S.E., & Malinak, J. (1989). The role of judgement calls in meta-analysis. *Journal of Applied Psychology,* 74, 259-264.

Weiss, H.M., & Adler, S. (1984). Personality and organizational behavior. *Research in Organizational Behavior,* 6,1-50.

Weiss, H.M., & Cropanzano, R. (1996). Affective events theory. *Research in Organizational Behavior,* 18, 1-74.

Weitz, J. (1952). A neglected concept in the study of job satisfaction. *Personnel Psychology,* 5, 201-205.

White, A.T., and Spector, P.E. (1987). An investigation of age related factors in the age-job satisfaction relationship. *Psychology and Aging,* 2, 261-265.

White, R.W. (1959). Motivation reconsidered : The concept of competence. *Psychological Review,* 66, 297-333.

Wiener, Y., & Vardi, Y. (1980). Relationships between job, organization and career commitment and work outcome – an integrative approach. *Organizational Behaviour and Human Performance,* 26, 81-96.

Wiley, J.W. (1996). Linking survey results to customer satisfaction and business performance. In A.I. Kraut (Ed.), *Organizational surveys* (pp. 330-359). San Francisco : Jossey-Bass.

Williams, C.R., & Livingstone, L.P. (1994). Another look at the relationship between performance and voluntary turnover. *Academy of Management Journal*, 37, 269-298.

Wood, R., Bandura, A., & Bailey, T. (1990). Mechanisms governing organizational performance in complex decision-making environments. *Organizational Behavior and Human Decision Processes*, 46, 181-201.

Wood, R.E., & Bandura, A. (1989). Impact of conceptions of ability on self-regulatory mechanisms and complex decision making. *Journal of Personality and Social Psychology*, 56, 407-415.

Wood, R.E., & Bandura, A. (1989). Social cognitive theory of organizaticnal management. Academy of Management Review, 14, 361-384.

Wood, R.E., & Locke, E.A. (1987). The relation of self-efficacy and grade goals to academic performance. *Educational and Psychological Measurement*, 47, 1013-1024.

Wotruba, T.R., & Tyagi, P.K. (1991). Met expectations and turnover in direct selling. *Journal of Marketing*, 55, 24-25.

Wright, T.A., & Bonett, D.G. (1993). Role of employee coping and performance in voluntary employee withdrawal : A research refinement and elaboration. *Journal of Management*, 19, 147-161.

Wunder, R.S., Dougherty, T.W., & Welsh, M.A. (1982). A causal model of role stress and employee turnover. *Academy of Management Proceedings*, K.H. Chung (ed.), 297-301.

Youngblood, S.A., Mobley, W.H., & Meglino, B.M. (1983). A longitudinal analysis of the turnover process. *Journal of Applied Psychology*, 68, 507-516.

Zenger, T.R. (1992). Why do employers only reward extreme performance. Examining the relationships among performance, pay and turnover. *Administrative Science Quarterly*, 37, 198-219.